Blame it on the

Scrumpy Tales from Somerset

Roger Evans

COUNTRYSIDE BOOKS
NEWBURY BERKSHIRE

COUNTRYSIDE BOOKS
3 Catherine Road
Newbury, Berkshire

To view our complete range of books
please visit us at
www.countrysidebooks.co.uk

ISBN 978 1 85306 762 4

Cover illustration by Mike Stringer
Cover design by Nautilus Design (UK) Ltd
Other illustrations by Pat Frost

Produced through The Letterworks Ltd., Reading
Typeset by Mac Style, Beverley, East Yorkshire
Printed by The Holywell Press Ltd., Oxford

Contents

1

A Somerset Childhood

Childhood reminiscences

I was fortunate enough to be born into those post war years with little traffic, when few risks existed for children roaming free from their parents and when orchards abounded in every corner of my home county of Somerset. Blessed with such freedom, and living within a mile of a dozen or so orchards, many of my happy childhood hours were spent wandering across fields and around the cider orchards which formed the very essence of Somerset's rural communities. Indeed there is nothing quite so quintessentially Somerset as cider.

Living on the edge of Bridgwater, my bedroom window looked over those childhood orchard playgrounds where grew such apple varieties as the bitter sharp Kingston Blacks, which produced an excellent late cider, and the crisp but dry Morgan Sweets, which were responsible for an earlier and much lighter offering. Sadly those orchards have long since disappeared, to be irrecoverably replaced with housing developments and motorway.

Long gone are those lichen covered twisted trunks where ivy hid the soft, downy nests of Jenny wrens, robins and blue tits. No longer do the apple trees stand in imperfect rows, trunks leaning this way and that, like churchyard gravestones failing the test of time, but so graciously permitting grazing sheep and cattle to reap the benefit of their angled poise where low down back-scratching surfaces display knots of wool collected on the roughened bark. The trees had themselves a 'half cidered up' look about them, like Dad's Army after a night out, almost in straight lines but unable to stand upright without leaning into some invisible prop.

You don't lose just an orchard when those trees are grubbed out, you lose a wildlife environment. You lose part of the social fabric of the rural communities, the skills and knowledge gathered across generations of farming families, lost forever.

Other losses have followed in the wake of change. No longer do the barn owls quarter the fields at dusk, feeding on voles which lived in the longer grasses within the orchards. No longer do the hay meadows offer that spring carpet of colours over which skylarks soared, lapwings tumbled and bats flittered at dusk. Nor do the rhynes and ditches abound with aquatic creatures which once provided endless hours of hunting for young lads with nets made from mother's discarded stockings.

All that remain are the West Country stories of yesteryear, in equal proportions of tragic and comic, and the memories of those carefree days of youth, exploring one's home territory and discovering at first hand the delights of local cider. Ah, that first taste of fresh young cider, as fresh and young as the lad being introduced to its delights, a raw novice, when the season's earliest croppers gave up their yield.

Read on and discover the lost world of Somerset cider.

Never to be forgotten, that first long secret drink of golden fire, juice of those valleys and of that time, wine of wild orchards, of plump red apples, and Rosie's burning cheeks.

Laurie Lee, Cider with Rosie

Pork and apple

Other memories survive, vivid memories of cider's effects on man and beast alike. Beasts? How do animals fit into those childhood recollections? As this story unfolds, so it will be revealed that it is not just man who loses his faculties under the influence of alcohol, but in the case of cider, the grazing animals suffer a similar fate.

Between my home and the River Parrett lies the hamlet of Dunwear and there on the corner of Plum Lane (fewer lanes could carry a more rural name) was a long, low, red brick barn forming the part of one boundary of a cider orchard. As with all farms in the area, the local farmer grew his own apple crop and in the autumn brewed his farmhouse cider. Once the juice had been extracted from the apples, the remaining pulp would be put into the orchards for the pigs to benefit from this additional food source.

On one particular occasion, there had been three days of rain after the pulp had been put out for the pigs, the pulp having been placed in an old metal bath in the heart of the orchard. The rainwater which collected in the bath had slowly been absorbed by the apple pulp and from the juices which settled therefrom a second batch of apple juice had been created, settling in the bottom of the bath.

Cider apples carry with them a natural yeast which allows the fermentation process to begin with no artificial intervention. And thus during the two or three weeks that it took for the pigs to munch their way down to the bottom of the bath, the juices gathered there had fermented themselves into a very rough but very natural cider. No doubt the pigs found this much to their taste for when I arrived, I witnessed one pig in an advanced state of drunkenness, leaning against the barn wall as its only means of support.

It was one very sad looking pig which slowly, over the course of the afternoon, delicately moving one trotter at a time, made its way to the end of the barn wall, never once standing up unaided. When the wall ran out, so the pig, with no further additional support, simply rolled over and there slept off the effects of its overindulgence. Had it been butchered the following day, there would surely have been little need for apple sauce to enhance the flavour. In similar fashion, Arthur Harris at Brean once had a sow which got into the pomace, the apple pulp, and it was three days before she was back on her feet.

At Dunkeswell, the American GIs, stationed there during the war, adopted a local pig and bought cider for it at the Royal Oak. Somehow they managed to train it to roll over on its back and open its mouth whilst they poured in the cider. By the time peace broke out and the GIs returned home, the pig was an alcoholic and refused to eat without its allowance of cider. Needless to say, it went to market shortly after VE Day.

Fellow author John Sparkes related to me how he once had a near miss with a bull which got itself 'cidered up'. In the years before John left school, he spent one Saturday morning gathering fallen apples and putting them into sacks in order to clear an area in the orchard for a football match. There, in the sacks, the apples spent the next month unattended and slowly fermenting.

John, at this time, was being taught to thatch. He was in the process of thatching a rick in a field where an old bull and a younger bull were tethered. Somehow the elder managed to slip its tether and from the top of the rick John was able to watch it get stuck into the sacks of fermenting apples. Drunk pigs may be humorous but drunk bulls can be downright dangerous.

Slowly the effects of the cider took control of the bull. Seeing the still tethered young bull, its challenger in the natural order of things, the older bull pawed the ground, dropped its head and charged the unmoving but nervous youngster. Fortunately for the younger bull, its elder was too intoxicated to charge straight and completely missed its young target. Not to be outdone, it looked for something else on which to expel its aggression.

There before it stood two brand new fowl houses complete with windows clean enough to be a mirror. And therein lay the problem. The bull looked at the first fowl house and saw its own reflection. Once more pawing the ground with head dipped in threatening pose, it challenged this unmoving intruder, which in turn was provocatively copying each and every threatening move.

Such bravado could not go unchecked and the drunken bull charged head first towards its rival. The fowl house proved to be no match. The bull simply crashed through unopposed. To the bull's complete surprise not only had the fowl house disappeared but, as if by magic, so had its cowardly challenger, clearly too timid to stay and fight. But then the bull noticed the second fowl house and, sure enough, on looking into the window, it spotted where the challenger had gone to ground. A second charge and further sounds of smashing glass and splintering timbers, and another fowl house bit the dust. But this time, so had the 'mirrored' bull which was nowhere to be seen. With that the bull slumped down, exhausted by its efforts, and drifted into a dream world of vanquished challengers whilst John seized the opportunity to safely descend from his viewing platform atop the rick and escape whilst the bull's radar was temporarily out of service.

Snobbing, scrumping and other illicit practices

Other childhood memories involved *scrumping* or *snobbing*, the local terms for pinching apples. At the time we were convinced of our ability as youngsters to outrun any farmer who discovered our presence. How we prided ourselves on never being captured. It is only with the benefit of adult hindsight that one realises the farmers had little interest in catching such errant youngsters. They simply frightened them off with the minimum expulsion of their own energy.

Whilst apple pinching was one innocent pastime, perhaps more serious was the one attempt I was involved in of establishing our own supply of cider. An old schoolfriend lived in a cottage tied to the local farm. Around the back of the cottage, in a low, red brick outhouse, with iron bars on the otherwise open windows, were stored large barrels, hogsheads of the farm produced cider.

Reaching through the bars, access to the barrels was simplicity itself. With the benefit of a penknife with one of those spikes for removing the stones from horses' hooves, we drilled a small hole in the end of the barrel through which the cider then began to pour. As young lads of eleven or twelve, we lacked the experience to fully consider the implications of our actions. We had drunk no more than a glass each when the error of our ways began to reveal itself.

To reach the barrels we had to stretch our arms to full length with shoulders pressing deeply into the iron bars of the window through which we worked. In such fashion we could just reach the lower part of the barrel end and at that point we drilled our hole. But we had given no consideration as to how we would stop the flow once it had started.

The cider kept pouring. At first it was easy, it was a slow flow, and by putting our glasses beneath the 'cider spring', we could capture the amber nectar, satisfy our thirst and just keep pace with the outflow. But after a couple of glasses it became increasingly difficult to determine just how we should stop the flow and avoid detection. With each successive glass, the problem became increasingly insurmountable until we reached that state of oblivion where we didn't really care. What happened thereafter is something of a blur. I seem to remember we simply left the problem unresolved. Somehow, as the afternoon progressed, it took on less and less significance!

A similar story of an adolescent attempt to raid a cider barn comes from Merv Pople, a former resident of Cossington. Merv was sixteen at the time and that was sufficiently long ago for it to be safe now to reveal his story. There was a dance at the Cossington village hall and Merv and his friend Keith were in attendance. To their surprise, one Wilfy Haggett turned up.

Now Wilfy was renowned for his cider which was stored in hogshead barrels in his garage. Realising that Wilfy, being at the dance, was not in attendance at home to safeguard his cider stocks, Merv and Keith set out on a late night raid.

Under cover of darkness they entered the garage where Wilfy kept his supplies and had filled a jar or two when they heard the sound of Wilfy unexpectedly arriving home. As quick as a couple of scurrying rats, Merv and Keith hid behind the barrels. Wilfy drove his car into the garage and locked the doors behind him with our two characters still inside.

Once they figured Wilfy was safely in the house, Merv and Keith realised their best attempt at an escape would be to climb up to just beneath the roof and then slide back some roof tiles to create an opening through which to climb. As they did so, a tile went into free fall, noisily sliding down over the other tiles before it crashed to the ground outside. That was enough to raise the alarm and by the time Merv and Keith were scurrying away into the darkness, Wilfy was already out there with his twelve bore shotgun threatening the death penalty on whoever it was that was disappearing into the dark beyond.

A happy ending – Merv was to return to that barn on a later date, invited with his Uncle Bob, who carried him home unconscious at the end of a night's imbibing. I guess Wilfy had either forgiven or forgotten Merv's previous transgression.

Adolescence

In my own adolescent years whilst visiting a farm at Fowler's Plot on the edge of the village of Chedzoy, I was introduced to *antique* cider. My choice of the word antique rather than vintage is quite deliberate. With an old friend, Dave Elson, I was visiting the home of Timmy Hansford. We were discussing the merits of cider when Timmy told us of a really old barrel recently discovered on the farm. The general opinion was that it was over a hundred years old, and could be proven to be at least eighty years in the barrel.

Our naive expectation was that this would prove to be a barrel of particularly strong cider, well mellowed in its oak container. Timmy warned us that it was not as we would expect and that he doubted if we were men enough to drink it. He knew we would rise to the challenge and we called for a pint apiece. Timmy offered us a thimbleful, a deliberately offensive quantity to young lads who thought they knew better but were still very soft at the edges.

We entered the gloom of the shed where the dust coated barrel lay innocently racked on its shelving. Hens pecked at the floor and swallows darted from darkened roof beams into the blinding sunlight with never a hint of pausing to adjust to the light. In the darkened barn, bare but for barrels on long benches and the rusting tools adorning the walls, we wiped the cobwebs from a deeply encrusted mug and by way of compromise, Timmy poured half a pint for us to share. Beneath the darting swallows, we each swigged in turn, but oh so briefly, from the jar.

Timmy was of course quite right. Whilst we were seduced by the thoughts of its strength and maturity, he knew that at least seventy years before it would have turned to vinegar. No sooner had the liquid passed out tongues, than it shot back in the opposite direction as the strongest acid ever to pass my lips opened its assault on my taste buds. It was truly dreadful but a useful lesson in the application of sell by dates – not that they existed in the latter days of the 19th century when the barrel was put to stand.

Such experiences were in my teenage years when the hedgerows in spring were thickly draped with mayflower blossom, like lace tablecloths, to be replaced in summer by the higher flowering elder, the lace cloth migrating up to the hedgerow canopy. Young buxom girls in white shorts cycled the lanes with picnic-holding wicker baskets strapped to their handlebars and cornfields competed to see which could claim to be the most densely spattered with bright red poppies. And the evening scent of wild honeysuckle filled the nostrils with a fragrant sense of well-being.

In winter months our thoughts turned to the dances we attended. Boys and girls arrived together but parted once inside the hall such that boys lined one side wall and clustered together, feet shuffling uncomfortably as we stared at and discussed the girls who lined the other side of the hall, contemplating which ones were the most likely to accept an advance. It was a long lonely walk back from one side to the other for those who chose unwisely.

Resurrectional experience

Another recollection of my youth dates back to the occasion when I had been on a late night drinking session with Martin whose surname will remain anonymous because his mother is still alive. This was Martin's first real experience with cider – the first time he had consumed several pints in one evening. His legs were seriously failing him and his brain was performing no better.

He failed to make it home that night, having collapsed unconscious between two tombstones in the local churchyard. It was a summer's night and so no harm came to him as he lay unnoticed and out of sight, sheltered from the early morning chill, between the stone capped tombs. And who knows to what depths Morpheus may descend when given favourable circumstances or what illusions may occur on resurfacing? As he awoke and looked around through a hazy drunken blur, seeing the surrounding tombstones, he was convinced that the resurrection day had come and he was the first to surface.

Flat on his back he stared skyward to see a police constable silhouetted against the early morning sun. 'OK lad, up you get and move along,' he commanded. Martin, still in his drunken stupor, and convinced this was a resurrectional experience, looked around him and responded in the vernacular – 'You wake they other buggers up first. They bin 'ere longer 'n I 'ave!'

> *No animal ever invented anything so bad as drunkenness – or so good as drink.*
>
> G. K. Chesterton, All Things Considered

2

The History of Cider

A pples are indigenous to England. One wild variety (Malus Silvestris) can be traced to Neolithic times but was too sharp to be edible and was probably cultivated by the Druids in order to grow their more significant mistletoe crop. But undoubtedly the practice of turning apples into alcohol goes back to a time before the history books first mention cider.

The Romans formalised the idea of apple orchards in Britain when their soldiers settled here, and there is evidence that the Saxons made some sort of cider. But it was the Normans who introduced cider making as an art, bringing new varieties such as Pearmains and Costards. In 1230, and the years shortly after, we can find local records of Bishop Jocelin of Bath accepting grants for cider presses and later receiving monies raised from the production of cider. By the end of the 13th century, cider formed an essential part of the rural economy.

Numerous wills throughout the 16th to 18th centuries make reference to hogsheads of cider indicating the importance attached to the value of cider as a commodity. And why not when the quality of water in those times was so variable. It was often safer to consume only cider rather than run the risk of illness associated with contaminated water. Indeed during the 17th century every man, woman and child would typically consume a quart a day.

Cider was cheap, plentiful and local. It lacked the high cost of tea and coffee which were the domain of the rich. By the 17th century cider had become the staple drink in the West Country with orchards planted across the region. It formed not only a part of the fabric of West Country social life but also a part of the system of payment for farm workers.

Cider versus cash

Up to two gallons a day could be consumed, but typically men were given five pints a day and women and boys two. In the summer months this would peak at a gallon or more at harvest time. We must remember that as recently as two hundred years ago most people worked on the land and that the quality of water was very poor. To contract some waterborne ailment might incapacitate the afflicted person to such an extent that no wages could be earned.

It was also part of the social life of the farm. The offering of a glass of cider to each and every visitor was as natural as it is today to offer a cup of tea. In my father's early days as a postman, it was quite expected that the postman delivering the mail would be offered a glass of cider with his morning delivery, and many of those postmen visited the farms even when there was no mail!

In similar fashion, baker's and butcher's carts would stop at each farm on their route and their drivers would be offered a glass. Our local paperman, when we lived in the village of Puriton, took his own supply, just in case. He would begin his round at one end of the village with a full firkin of cider and finish at our end with it empty. We lived at the wrong end of the village!

But back to those days of yore. At harvest time, the gallons of cider consumed were taken over the course of a long hot, sweaty day of haymaking, from six in the morning until ten at night. It is easy to imagine a labourer out there amongst the other workers, drunkenly flailing his scythe around until everyone was legless, himself metaphorically and the rest literally. But a gallon of cider over a sixteen hour day is only half a pint an hour. And they'd be sweating off that amount for most of the day. Indeed, at harvest time, not to have offered a ration of cider was tantamount to declaring that no casual labour was needed since this was one of the great incentives for the extra help required.

This practice of imbibing cider at harvest time still continues to a lesser degree even today. Certainly during the last war, when the nation was digging for victory, harvest workers looked for their ration. One account of a wartime worker has him travelling from farm to farm trying to find work. Everywhere was empty until he came to a farm at which all the agricultural workers in the area had congregated – and every one of them was to be found in the cider cellar. Their day commenced with collecting the eggs and milking the cows, then in for their lunch and off to the cellar to finish lunch with a glass or two of cider. That cider drinking somehow saw them through until milking time in the evening!

Half gallon stone cider jars encased in protective baskets of willow or wooden firkins, small half gallon barrels, would be taken into the fields and left in the rhynes or streams to keep cool. As the day progressed, the wives brought out bread, cheese and yet more cider. The payment in kind of cider as part of the wages became somewhat formalised and a labourer's wage would perhaps be seven shillings in cash plus a shilling's worth of cider.

> *Yes, cider and tinned salmon are the staple diet of the agricultural classes.*
>
> Evelyn Waugh, Scoop, Book 1

Gallons of cider were consumed during the long hot hours of harvesting.

A cider bounty

It's hard to imagine anyone offering a hogshead of cider as a bounty payment but that was the case in 1775. Four years earlier Arthur Young, the agricultural commentator, described Sedgemoor as a sea in winter and a disgrace to the nation. Across the country farmland was being improved and increased in value. King's Sedgemoor was ripe for such an improvement.

A bill was presented to Parliament for the drainage and enclosure of King's Sedgemoor. But it appears the bill put before Parliament was different in form on twenty counts to that explained to the local people. The discovery of the fraud led to widespread violence. A man working as a land surveyor, and acting on behalf of those whose interests lay in the success of the bill, was threatened with his life and a bounty put on his head of a hogshead of cider.

Cider Truck Act

Towards the end of the 19th century, the clergy were growing increasingly concerned about the effects of the cider given to farm workers in the form of wages. The increasing abuse of cider helped to fuel the Temperance Movement. In 1887 the Truck Act stopped the payment of wages in kind but it failed to impact upon cider. The practice of offering cider as a payment was deeply inculcated in the rural way of life and was to continue much longer.

But what of the quality of the cider used for wages. It was certainly inferior to that which would be consumed by the farmer or his family. It was the cider made from the second pressing. Suffice it to say that the best quality cider came from the first pressing. The second pressing produced a much weaker and lower quality drink.

Since in many cases only the worst cider was given to the labourers, there was often a detrimental effect on the general health of the local labour force. It was considered quite noticeable in some villages that the elderly ladies could out-lift the elderly men, such was the effect of rough cider drunk daily during a working lifetime. It was generally agreed that if the second pressing cider was any worse, you couldn't drink it – and any better, they wouldn't give it to you.

After the First World War, mechanisation on farms increased, bringing with it the risk of serious injury if the operators had been drinking. With the men returning from the war now favouring cash instead of payment in kind, so the consumption of cider and its use as a wage diminished and with it the number of orchards and much of the social way of life.

Cider and the revenue

Rents and tithes were often paid in cider. As far back as the 13th century, cider formed part of some tax returns. This was never a popular practice but as part of a tithe system, whereby one tenth of everything produced was to be given to the lord of the manor or the church, it would have been natural for cider to be part of that tithe. What was unnatural, and certainly caused great hostility, was the cider tax introduced by an Act of Parliament in 1763.

The tax was set at four shillings per hogshead, anything from forty to sixty gallons according to the region. But the most controversial aspect was the additional powers that came with the act which allowed private premises to be searched. The reaction was universal condemnation and rarely has the introduction of new legislation created such hostile feeling, exceeding even that of the Poll Tax in more recent years. Not a farm in the county was safe.

No longer was an Englishman's home his castle. At any time, day or night, his house could be searched. Pitt the Elder protested against the police having power to invade a home and in one tirade he declared: 'The poorest man in his cottage may bid defiance to all the force of the Crown. It may be frail; its roof may leak; the wind may blow through it; the storms may enter; the rain may enter – but the King of England cannot enter; all his forces dare not cross the threshold of the ruined tenement!' And hence was popularised the expression that an Englishman's home is his castle.

Charles Kemys Tynte, resident of Halswell House near Bridgwater and one of Somerset's MPs, was so incensed with the act, partly because of a smear campaign against him which suggested he had not tried hard enough to get it repealed, that he published a declaration of his opposition to it. Despite his poor state of health, he was carried to the House of Commons wrapped in blankets in order not to miss his opportunity to vote for it to be set aside.

The act was repealed in 1766. As a result there was great rejoicing across the county with bonfires blazing, church bells ringing, and bands parading and playing in their local towns and villages. Amidst this air of festivity, huge quantities of cider were consumed.

If all be true that I do think
There are five reasons we should drink;
Good wine, a friend, or being dry,
Or lest we should be by and by;
Or any other reason why.
Henry Aldrich, 1689

3

Cider Making

Art versus science

Good cider making is an art and not a science. Yet when the process is taken on by the larger producers, the art is removed and science takes over. As an example, with 'natural' cider, no yeast is added to the process. The yeast used is that which is naturally present on the skin of the apples or lingering from an earlier batch, and is therefore unpredictable in how rapidly it will promote fermentation. The brewer needs to keep a watchful eye to determine when to halt proceedings.

Some large manufacturers kill off the natural apple yeast and add their own in order to eliminate variability, replacing nature and art with science. I remember watching a tankerload of apple concentrate from Spain arrive at the Taunton Cider Company at the very time the company was promoting Taunton as the place where cider making was still an art.

This company had started life in Norton Fitzwarren in 1911 and grew to produce 19 million gallons per year. But it was never a match for the true local cider. It was factory cider with imported concentrates and fizz added – with artificial colourings and flavouring.

True cider, or Scrumpy, is one hundred percent natural and there has always been a competitive spirit between Devon and

Somerset with each considering their own county's cider to be superior and neither giving a consideration to that produced in Hereford. In 1902 it was a Somerset cider which won that year's national championship prize. The Devon producers, not unexpectedly, declared the winning brew to be fit only for women and children to drink, such was the rivalry.

Fortunately, just as with real ales, locally produced cider is slowly making a welcome comeback and names such as Rich's, Perry's and Wilkins, along with numerous others, are a byword for good quality, natural cider.

Walking on water

I well remember the occasion when, with a group of friends from the Bridgwater Carnival Committee, I was a guest of the Taunton Cider Company, and we were treated to a factory tour and cider tasting. First we had a meal complemented with cider or apple juice as the only choice of beverages. This was followed by a cider tasting lesson in the different types of cider.

However, not all of our party enjoyed cider and so for those who didn't, there was the problem of what to do with the unwanted samples. Never one to miss an opportunity, Arthur, one of our party, came to the rescue and helped out all of those who preferred to leave the cider by finishing their samples for them. But Arthur was to pay the price as we journeyed home.

We had only gone a couple of miles towards Bridgwater when Arthur needed to answer the call of nature. The coach driver pulled into the roadside where a short grass verge separated the coach from the ditch. Because of the time of year, this was full to the brim and covered in a thick blanket of duckweed, giving the impression of a solid surface level with the grass verge. All of us on board could see how easily Arthur, the worse the wear for an overindulgence during the tasting session, could mistake the ditch as solid ground in the dim glow cast from the coach's interior lights.

'Mind the ditch Arthur. It's right in front of you!' I called. 'It's all right, I can see the hedge,' replied Arthur. The fact that he could see the hedge, which was on the other side of the ditch, told us all that he could not see what was directly beneath his feet. One small step for one man and Arthur was in the ditch up to his armpits, and covered from head to foot in stinking duckweed.

It was a very embarrassed and dripping wet Arthur who climbed back onto the coach, looking up into the face of the chief of Bridgwater's police force who was one of our party. 'I think it might be best if you sit on the steps,' advised the Chief Inspector. And that was where Arthur spent the next ten miles as we headed homeward.

We were probably about a mile and a half from Arthur's home when his wife called out, 'Can you stop the coach here please, driver?' The driver duly pulled in and Arthur's wife went to the front. 'Right. Off you get. You walk from here!' Arthur, with his tail between his legs, alighted, the coach door closed and his good lady walked back to her seat muttering 'Perhaps that will give him time to sober up and dry out a bit before I get my hands on him!'

The orchards

As with the cider making process, so have orchards suffered through 'progress'. The once forty trees per acre have been replaced with bush trees at two hundred and forty per acre reflecting the need to mechanise and reduce cost with less consideration for quality. The old style of orchard was based on mostly standard trees which allowed sheep and geese to graze beneath their boughs, their droppings forming a natural part of the harvest as the fallen cider apples were gathered in.

Good natural cider is made from English apples from English orchards. Fine old names such as Kingston Black, Dabinett, Yarlington Mill, Stoke Red, Harry Masters and Morgan Sweet were synonymous with farm life and cider making. Tom Putts were one of the most attractive apples, a deep rich red which looked quite delicious and year after year caught youngsters out with its bittersharp taste, causing the cheeks to pucker and eyes to squint as the oversharp pulp was spat out until every last lingering acidic torment had been dispelled.

Jilly Goolden on the BBC's *Food and Drink* programme once sang the praises of the Kingston Black, named after its home village of Kingston St Mary near Taunton, as probably the best cider apple – 'This has got muscles. This has got brawn. This has got a hairy chest. I think it's gorgeous.' And I think it's wonderful that someone can get so excited by such a simple item as a cider apple and describe its merits based on its taste rather than its aesthetic appearance on a supermarket shelf.

Which apples to grow would depend on the taste of the farmer and the need to provide an all year round supply of cider. Kingston Blacks produce a cider with fine keeping qualities which will take it through to the next summer. These are ready to harvest much later in the season than Morgan Sweets which crop earlier and produce a cider which needs to be drunk when relatively young. But this early cropper nicely fills the gap between the cider from last year's later crops running out and their new crops being ready for consumption.

Maintaining standards

Orchards grow old and need to be replaced. Sadly when times are changing, good care and maintenance of those aspects of farming which have a longer payback period are often the first to be neglected. Such was the case in 1896 when many orchards were aged and in a state of decline. Standards in cider making had slipped to such an extent that the Gold Medal for cider remained unawarded at the Bath and West Show. But out of this depressing situation was born the Long Ashton Research Station, set up under the name of the National Fruit and Cider Institute. Over the decades that institute has achieved much in improving the quality of good local cider and in achieving market place recognition for cider as a quality beverage in stark contrast to the low grade product experienced towards the end of the 19th century.

Despite the efforts at Long Ashton, orchards continued their decline. In a hundred years Somerset orchards have diminished from over ten thousand hectares to just over one thousand. The disappearance of cider as a form of wage brought about much of this decline which was worsened by the introduction of mechanisation. In the decades after the last war, the government was issuing grants to those who grubbed out their apple trees. In recent years, that policy has been reversed and grants are now available for planting new orchards.

Harvesting the apples

The traditional way to harvest cider apples has always been to leave them to fall, perhaps with a little help from a long pole or by shaking the tree. Then like a gentle roll of thunder the apples hit the ground ready to be gathered in. This means that collecting the apples would be quite late in the year, perhaps when the heavy dew from the chilled November nights still lay on the ground.

Collecting apples by hand from the floor of the orchard can be quite back-breaking work and was normally carried out by women and children, the men having to bend further to reach the ground. Thistles and stinging nettles were a common problem. Avoiding wasps feeding off the rotting fruits was another. Even those rotten apples, so loved by the autumn wasps, were included in the gathering process, as long as they were brown and not yet turned black.

Generally speaking the apples would not be washed or cleansed in any way although today's higher standards require otherwise. Twigs and bits of branches would be removed but bird droppings were left to join the rest of the crop. Using withy baskets on the Somerset Levels, or ash stave baskets on Exmoor, the apples were collected into pecks, baskets carrying about twenty pounds. These would be transferred into bigger three peck baskets and taken away to where they were collected in large piles convenient for the press. It was, and is, quite usual for the collected apples to be left for a couple of weeks to concentrate their sugar content and flavour.

Milling

The apples once collected would normally be taken up to a loft from where they could be fed into the top of the mill. For the smaller producer, everything was done at ground floor level. The actual cider making process is much the same today. Before the juice is squeezed from the apples, they need to be milled. Here the apples are chopped but not crushed since it is important not to lose the juices at this stage, but to save them within the flesh until the pressing commences.

The bad, or black, fruit is removed before milling, the end product of which is a pulpous mass referred to as pomace (from the French for apple – pomme).

Cider pressing where the juice is gently extracted.

Extracting the juice

Once milled, the pomace is taken to the press in buckets or on pomace scoops where it is laid down with alternate layers of straw for the traditionalist or wrapped in cheese cloth for the modernists. It may be formed in cloths to make cakes and the cakes into cheeses, perhaps a ton at a time, and the cheeses are then stacked before pressing. It takes some skill to stack the cheeses correctly to ensure even pressure across the stack. When high enough, they are topped out with a large block of oak to spread the pressure and then pressed.

The colour of the cider is in part enhanced by the straw but additional colour is quite often added with beetroot, blackberries or elderberries being thrown in. One cider producer, short of apples, bought in a load which had been individually wrapped in blue paper. He removed hundreds of the wrappers but got fed up and threw in the rest with the wrappers still on. The cider finished quite unsaleable with a rather unusual blue tint.

Mrs Perry, of Perry's Cider fame, told me how her father, William Evans, added beetroot to give his cider extra colour. He only produced for domestic consumption, for family and visitors, and found the addition of extra beetroot quite beneficial. Tested with a blindfold, I doubt that anyone could have told the difference between the cider produced with no beetroot and that produced with a significant dose. But with eyes wide open, the cider enhanced with the beetroot had a bright red colour, creating the perception of a health warning. Visitors were reluctant to drink more than a minimal amount of this lethal appearing liquid, which suited Mr Evans down to the ground in those post war years where rationing still applied.

The presses, diesel driven hydraulic mechanisms these days, used to be powered by man or horse using a stone press. The stack was pressed for a day or two – a process not to be rushed. John Philips in a poem he wrote in 1708 gives advice on how this should be achieved:

> *Be cautious next a proper Steed to find,*
> *Whose Prime is past; the vigorous Horse disdains*
> *Such servile Labours, or, if forc'd, forgets*
> *His past Atchievements, and victorious Palms.*
> *Blind Bayard rather, worn with Work, and Years,*
> *Shall roll th' unweildy Stone; with sober Pace*
> *He'll tread the circling Path 'till dewy Eve,*
> *From early Day-spring, pleas'd to find his Age*
> *Declining, not unuseful to his Lord.*

Recycled pomace

Once finished, the pomace was fed to the livestock or scattered in the orchard. I have lost count of the times when members of the farming community have related to me stories of animals intoxicated this way. Horses, cows and pigs being the most common, but also pheasants feeding off it would become quite drunk and, as a consequence, extremely easy to catch.

Cows in particular suffer since they have three stomachs and thus the apples have ample time to ferment internally. The theme of drunken pigs, when linked with drunken humans, leads me nicely into a poem I have heard told across the county when addressing various audiences. Sadly I know not of its origin and am unable to give credit to the author. Indeed it is now so well known as to perhaps be considered 'traditional'.

> *One evening last September, as I do well remember,*
> *I was walking down the street in drunken pride*

31

When I fell down in the gutter 'cos my legs went all a stutter
Then a pig came down and lay there by my side.

As I lay there in the gutter, thinking thoughts I should not utter,
A stranger passing by did softly say
'You can tell a man who boozes by the company he chooses'
And with that the pig got up and walked away!

Guy Gibbs of Biddisham once told me of the problems which occurred when cattle were allowed into the orchard when the fallen apples were into the rotting stage. The cows would eat them quite happily but the digestive process led to contaminated milk. Indeed the milk produced the following day had a brown tinge, making it quite unsaleable. A similar problem also resulted when the cattle were put into a field with wild garlic in flower. The milk produced was flavoured with the garlic and whilst suitable for cheese making would soon be rejected for drinking purposes.

In centuries past a second pressing of the apple pomace was normally taken after soaking the already squeezed pomace in water for a few days. This second pressing produced a much inferior cider, often referred to as ciderkin. Once again John Philips gives advice:

Some, when the Press, by utmost Vigour screw'd,
Has drain'd the pulpous Mass, regale their Swine
With the dry Refuse; thou, more wise shalt steep
Thy Husks in Water, and again employ
The pondrous Engine. Water will imbibe
The small Remains of Spirit, and acquire
A vinous Flavour; this the Peasants blith
Will quaff, and whistle, as thy tinkling Team
They drive, and sing of Fusca's radiant Eyes,
Pleas'd with the medly Draught. Not shalt thou now

Reject the Apple-Cheese, tho' quite exhaust;
Ev'n now 'twill cherish, and improve the Roots
Of sickly Plants; new Vigor hence convey'd
Will yield an Harvest of unusual Growth.
Such Profit springs from Husks discreetly us'd!

In these lines we find reference to that second pressing and its value in quenching the thirst of the peasants. I earlier made reference to the quality of this second pressing with the comment that if the quality were any better the farmer would sell it and any worse you couldn't drink it. And here we have John Philips from three hundred years ago confirming the practice and also advising the use of the 'pulpous Mass' to improve the roots of sickly plants.

Fermenting the juice

The juice, once extracted, is fed into casks ready for the fermentation process. These were traditionally wooden barrels, hogsheads, of over fifty gallons. The juice is then left to ferment. No yeast is added, the natural yeast ensuring a slow process taking weeks or even months to mature. During this time fumes are given off and it was the presence of these fumes which led to so many stories of animal and bird skeletons in the finished cider. It is true that rats occasionally fell in and roosters foolish enough to perch over the vats could be overcome by the fumes and loosen their grip. These extra bodies would often be evident at the bottom of the vats when it came to cleaning time.

It was not only farmers who brewed their own cider. Often the clergy produced their own supplies, perhaps from apples collected as a tithe. In one Somerset story, the local cider-making vicar, partway through delivering his Sunday sermon from the pulpit, was interrupted by one of his workers rushing

33

into the church shouting 'Vicar, 'tis all bubblin' over!' with which the vicar left his congregation mid-sermon to dash home and address the problem.

Drinking

Cider is a natural product. Its quality and appearance is therefore somewhat unpredictable. The apple variety, weather and type of ground all contribute to the variation in the finished item. Traditional cider is often cloudy, not being filtered. Sampling is an important part of the process and is something of an art. But naturally the odd worker will participate in clandestine sampling activities. One man who worked at Coate's in Nailsea was caught drinking on the job, earning himself instant dismissal from the managing director. The victim accepted his punishment graciously recognising that he had been fairly caught and justly dismissed but was still cheeky enough to ask if he could finish the bottle first.

The drinking of cider has always been a sociable activity. In the farmhouse, it would be a rare visitor indeed who was not invited to share a glass. For the workers it was a moment at the end of the day when they could sit together and quench their thirsts. Often in these gatherings, it would be a capacious two handled mug which would be passed around, the large handles aiding the passing and helping to form a natural bond between those who shared the experience. A few such mugs can occasionally be seen with three handles and often they will have the Farmer's Prayer scripted on the side. The *Somerset County Herald* of 23rd August 1924 makes the following reference to cider drinking: 'A Somerset native brought up anywhere near the cider producing areas of the county would not think of drinking cider out of a glass if there was a cup close handy. Not likely! Cider is a drink to be taken out of a cup ... Besides who can get a comfortable drink out of a half pint glass! And what Somerset farmer would drink cider out of a cup with one handle! How could he hand it around to those seated with him in the chimney corner? No, a two handled cup, please, if not a three handled one as we used to have on our farm when I was a lad.'

4

An Apple a Day

Sea voyages

The ability of cider to benefit both body and soul is matched anecdote for anecdote with those that relate the detrimental effect of an excess of cider. That there is a positive side to this beverage is beyond doubt and its efficacy was recognised many centuries ago.

In the early days of global exploration, when ships went to sea for months or years at a time, the importance of having sufficient fresh water cannot be underestimated. Fresh water, beer and even cider were of tremendous importance. Fresh water does not keep long at sea, especially in warmer climes. Beer keeps longer and cider, depending on the apple variety, keeps the longest of them all. So it was not the alcoholic effect of cider which made it so popular but its keeping qualities. In addition it also contains vitamin C, important in the prevention of scurvy, perhaps the mariners' most common ailment.

> *We drink one another's healths and spoil our own.*
> Jerome K. Jerome

Cider – the cure all

Apart from scurvy, the medicinal effects of cider have long been a good excuse for taking the occasional jar. As a child I remember the popularity of mulled cider with a drop of ginger as a cure for the common cold or influenza. Rheumatism or the 'screws' are generally accepted across the county as cured by cider; likewise acne. Even articles in *The Lancet* extolled the virtues of cider for rheumatism and gout and recommended doctors to get their gouty patients to switch from beers and wine to cider.

> *Cider does relax the belly ... aid concoction, depress vapours, resist melancholy, spleen, pleurisy, strangury, and being sweetened with sugar abate inveterate colds.*
>
> John Evelyn, Sylva – Pomona, 1664

Longevity

Of course cider in excess has a detrimental effect just as any other form of alcohol. It is no coincidence that rough cider is nicknamed 'Gut Rot'. But who can say whether or not cider prolongs or shortens life. There is many a farm labourer to reach a ripe old age but perhaps that is the result of hard and honest toil, reaping the benefits of the open air, free from the city stress. Farming communities undoubtedly benefit from a more natural diet with plenty of fresh meat and vegetables.

The cider drinking communities of Devon, at least, are convinced of the efficacious nature of their local cider as the following traditional drinking song from that county tells us:

> *I were brought up on cider,*
> *And I be a hundred and two.*
> *But still that be 'nuthin when you come to think*

37

Me father and mother be still in the pink.
And they were brought up on cider
Of the rare old Tavistock brew,
And me Granfer drinks quarts
For he's one of the sports
That were brought up on cider too.

There is a lovely story from the village of Burtle where it is claimed the villagers' longevity is due entirely to their daily consumption of cider. In 1839 when the village church was built, we are told that the villagers lived so long, they had to shoot the first three to get the graveyard started!

In another story relating to that same graveyard, one villager had it included in his will that when he was buried, he was to be laid to rest with his stone jar full of cider to help him on his journey and with all the cash in the house to help to pay his way. Prior to the funeral, his friends gathered in his parlour where he was laid out with the coffin still open to allow everyone to pay their last respects.

As his old drinking partners gathered around him, one of his old mates counted the money carefully placed at his side, took a cheque book from his pocket and made out a cheque to the same value. Putting the coins in his pocket and the cheque between the fingers of the corpse, he declared: 'That were always one of his good points. He were always willin' to change a cheque for his old mates. And he never minded sharing his cider with anyone.' And with that the jar was passed in traditional fashion, each in turn toasting their late friend who was later buried with an empty jar and a cheque.

The constant use of this liquor ... hath been found by long experience to avail much to health and long life; preserving the drinkers of it in their full strength and vigour even to very old age.
John Worlidge, A Treatise of Cider, 1676

5

Social History and Traditions

Wassail

On farms in particular, the sharing of cider has long since been part of the social fabric of life and the bond from sharing is strengthened, as we have seen, by the use of a two handled or even three handled mug which makes it easier to pass from one drinker to the next, almost as an act of communion. In winter months, cider was used to warm the body. On those raw winter's evenings when the frost and mist chilled the very bones, what better way to warm the cockles of the heart than to quaff a mug of hot cider, steam hissing as the hot iron mulling rod was taken from the fire and immersed in the jar? The addition of cloves or various spices added to the sense of comfort and well being.

The best known cider-related tradition, and one of the oldest surviving Somerset customs, is that of wassailing on the Old Twelfth Night, 17th January each year. Twelfth Night is generally considered to be 6th January but in 1752 the calendar was adjusted resulting in an eleven day shift. Traditions such as wassailing were so deep in the culture of Somerset folk that it was felt important to continue the practice on the same night each year despite the calendar change, hence 17th January.

The word wassail comes from the Anglo Saxon 'waes hael' – good health to you. The tradition continued at Walton until the 1970s and now survives most notably at the Butchers Arms at Carhampton (pronounced Cram'ton). The wassailing ceremony is carried out in the orchard where the youngest person attending places cake or toast soaked in cider in the forks of a tree, traditionally the oldest tree, and then a bucket of cider spiced with nutmeg and ginger is poured onto the roots and the wassailing song begins.

Oh apple tree we wassail thee
And happily wilt thou bear,
For the Lord doth know where we shall be
Till apples another year.

To bloom well and to bear well
So merry let us be,
Let every man take off his hat
And shout out to th'old apple tree.

The following chorus is then shouted:

Old apple tree! We wassail thee!
And hoping thou will bear
Hatsful, capsful, three bushel bagsful
And a little heap under the stair.

This is immediately followed by the traditional three cheers and gun shot is fired through the branches of the apple trees to frighten away the evil spirits and ensure a prosperous crop in the ensuing year. All present then retire to the bar for a night's serious celebration.

In centuries past, the farm labourers would tour the farms in this fashion and we can only imagine the amount of cider packed away by those chaps as they carried out this important duty.

Gun shot is fired through the branches to ward off evil spirits.

Harvest Home

Another tradition of sharing the fruits of one's labour with one's fellow man is that of the Harvest Home suppers. These come at the end of the harvest season after the last bale has been safely gathered in. In former years, there was no set date for such events, it was all arranged once the back of the harvest was broken. Then a harvest wain, or wagon, would be bedecked with branches and flowers and paraded through the streets on the way to the Harvest Home and the villagers would process to the banqueting area.

But such are the scale of these events today, where over a thousand people can sit down to dinner, that they have become all day affairs. The date is established well in advance and it doesn't really matter if the harvest isn't completely in as long as the marquee, the caterers and entertainers are all booked. And then of course the required number of tickets must be sold to make the event viable, unlike yesteryear when admission was free as a thank you to all those whose efforts had helped to bring in the harvest.

Excellent Harvest Home suppers still take place. Mark and East Brent provide good examples. Long tables within the marquees are laid out with ample wholesome fare, cold meats, hot meats and plenty of vegetables, and all washed down with liberal quantities of beer and cider. The interior of the marquee is draped with ivy ropes, hoops and banners. The purpose of the supper is perhaps lost these days, being better remembered in the Harvest Festival service now practised in most country churches. It does, however, serve as a convenient annual opportunity for the whole local community to gather.

One of the luckiest villages must have been Burtle which has its own Silver Band, a musical group with a tradition dating back generations. Sadly, whilst the band lives on, the Harvest Home in Burtle died out in 1970. John Sparkes told me how the village bobby, Bob Vickery, would turn a blind eye to the goings on at the Harvest Home. One farmer staggering out of the marquee just after midnight was asked by Bob how he was to get home. When the farmer declared that he had his car in the field, the policeman remarked how lucky that was because he'd never be able to walk home the state he was in!

Another character from the same village was Harry Whitcombe who on falling off his bike one day, after a jar too many, went head first over the handlebars and into a hedge near the post office. Whilst extracting himself from the hedge, he was asked, by an apparently well meaning but rather unwise lady, if he had fallen off his bike. 'Naw,' he replied, 'I always gits off like this.'

Cider pub traditions

The Athelney Inn in the heart of Sedgemoor was once a well established old cider house supporting the usual traditional pub games such as skittles and darts. It could also boast a most unusual game which required a black wooden disc to be fixed to the ceiling, about the size of a dinner plate. Two players then tossed coins so that they struck the black disc before descending to land as heads or tails. Ten points were scored for heads and one for tails. Each player in turn had to decide whether or not to toss again, the target being to get the closest to thirty-one without 'busting', in similar fashion to scoring twenty-one in pontoon. The game was played on the basis of the best of three rounds with the loser paying for a quart of cider for the victor – hence the name 'Tossing for Quarts'. The winner was then challenged by the next player in turn.

Cider salesmen of many years ago would take a small barrel as a free sample to pubs such as the Athelney Inn. On one such visit the salesman was presenting a barrel which had been produced as an experimentally strong cider, perhaps not to everybody's palate – but the market needed to be tested. The landlord immediately supplied a pint to his most regular cider drinker for an opinion. The drinker declared that it lacked body, he preferred something stronger and the salesman departed a disappointed man.

A few days later, to his surprise, the salesman received a sizeable order in the post from the landlord concerned. Enquiring later as to why the unexpected change of fortune had come about, he was told by the landlord that the regular cider drinker had downed two more pints of the same and had promptly fallen off his stool – for the first time in his life, he had been carried home.

Dead drunk

In another story of a drinker unable to get home, George Moore, a Nether Stowey undertaker, had working with him a particularly large man. At the end of one night's drinking the employee was too drunk to stand, let alone get home unaided. George, being the caring employer he was, felt honour bound to take the man home. However, the employee was far too heavy to carry and the only transport George had available was his hearse. With the help of three or four others, the unconscious employee was placed prostrate in the rear of the hearse. His delivery to his home came as a complete shock to his wife who misinterpreted the actual state of her husband's health as she was faced with his body apparently laid to rest.

Smoked husbands

There is a charming story of a farming family from just outside Athelney whose father had died[1]. The local vicar was met in a

---

1 *Somerset Year Book,* 1930

lane by the son of the family who enquired when it would be convenient to bury his father. Having offered his condolences the vicar asked the son when his father had died. 'Why, sir, he died about three months ago,' replied the son who proceeded to explain how his father had inconveniently died at harvest time, when the work was at the busiest, and there had been no time to bury him.

The mother of the family saw to the necessary arrangements and had her husband's lean body placed in the chimney, with a knob of salt in each eye and one in his mouth. There he was slowly smoked and preserved for a more convenient occasion. The now apparent urgency to bury him resulted from an unexpected visit by a friend. This unsuspecting visitor arrived to spend some time with his old mate. The family, unaware of the stranger's ignorance of the father's death, directed him to the chimney, assuming he was there to pay his last respects. There to his horror he came face to face with the corpse. An attempt at a rapid exit resulted in a fall over the front doorstep and a broken arm for his trouble. So mother decided the burial was now well overdue.

The nail-swallowing baby

The story of another mother, but one perhaps unsuited to her parental role, comes from the Quantock Hills. The lady concerned had several children and a bad drinking habit. More was spent on her cider than on food for the children. As a result of her frequent drunken bouts, she was well known to the local doctor who had long since tired of her incessant concerns over the health of her offspring, of whom at least one would be suspected of some imagined medical condition at any one time.

On one such occasion, the woman concerned arrived in a panic stricken state at the home of a neighbour. She demanded the doctor be called to her youngest child who was at serious risk of losing her poor little life as the result of swallowing a bag of nails. The neighbour telephoned the doctor who then spoke to the distraught mother. Asked what the problem was, the mother explained how she had purchased a bag of nails and now they were gone. Only the child had been in the room with the nails at the time and only the child consuming the nails could account for their disappearance.

The doctor explained that had the child swallowed one nail, the experience would be sufficiently unpleasant that he was convinced it would not have continued to consume the rest of the bag. The mother accused him of incompetence and questioned how he could know without examining the child. Offended by these remarks and now concluding the woman was suffering once again from an overindulgence of cider, he asked her how she could be so certain that the child had swallowed the nails. The woman replied, ''Cos she do rattle when I do shake 'er!' The phone was slammed down and the doctor retired to his otherwise peaceful Sunday break.

The challenge

A lovely story of a Crewkerne man who was a cider drinker of some renown was recorded in the *Somerset County Herald* on 23rd August 1924. The man had a reputation for his ability to consume large volumes of cider in a short space of time. He was legendary and his fellow drinkers were proud to boast of his prowess and wallow in the reflected glory. And so it was that on the occasion of a 'foreigner' from the Midlands being in their bar, and the visitor discussing the local cider, the man's fellow drinkers boasted how their friend was so good he could polish off a gallon without pausing for breath.

The visitor found these tales hard to swallow and challenged the authenticity of the claims being made on the absent man's behalf. But conveniently the very man of whose prowess they boasted arrived at the pub and the gauntlet was thrown down. A wager of a shilling was suggested on whether or not he could drink a gallon in one go.

There was a long expectant pause as the man considered the situation. He was actually uncertain as to whether he could achieve it. The wager was tempting but not without some risk. Having deliberated for some while he declared, 'I bain't zo zure. But let I go out for a minit or two and I'll tell 'ee.' On his return, he smiled and declared he was prepared to accept the challenge. A gallon of cider was drawn from the barrel, the man threw back his head and down went the cider. The wager had been fairly won and all present were well impressed.

The stranger, however, suspected there was something untoward in the man's earlier behaviour. Why had he gone out the back for five minutes or so? Was there some trickery involved? He challenged the local man and demanded an explanation. The cider drinker replied, 'Well, zur, 'tis like this, zur. I weren't quite zure I could do it for I'd a goodish drop down in the vield so I thought I'd try it out virst and I up wi' a gallon jar and empt'd 'en. Then I knowed I could win thic zhilling.'

6

Cider on the Farm

Fowl play

Chatting over a cup of tea in the farmhouse kitchen one evening, Guy Gibbs reflected on the years when cider was made on his Biddisham farm. He also mused on the days of his youth when as youngsters 'fowl play' was practised on the chickens. It is well understood that by taking a chicken and placing its head under its wing, as it does when roosting, and then gently swinging the chicken to and fro, sleep can be induced.

Guy's special trick was to take a number of chickens, feed them with the required dosage of home brewed cider, tuck their heads under their wings, and then place them on a plank of wood and set them adrift, floating gently towards the middle of the duckpond. The poor chickens would wake some while after, presumably wondering how on earth they had managed to get themselves marooned in the middle of the pond and no doubt contemplating what a hell of a party it must have been!

The power of telecommunications

I was delivering a talk on cider related stories one evening when a member of the audience told me of Tommy Lovell who was a farm worker of the old fashioned kind. Tommy was one of those farm labourers who still liked to have his drop of cider when it came to harvest time. He was employed by Mr King who farmed at Bishop's Lydeard and possessed a threshing machine. It was Tommy's job to go wherever Mr King sent him with his crew of two labourers.

Tommy was on a customer's farm one day and the threshing machine was well into the crop. He and his team of two had laboured hard throughout the morning and they each had a whistle to wet when they stopped for lunch. So off they went to the Lethbridge Arms where the cider went down a treat, and perhaps Tommy had more than was appropriate for someone supervising a threshing machine. But no matter, Tommy was confident as to his ability and took his crew back to the farm where they once more set about completing the task.

Tommy had received no instructions as to where he was to go next and so was looking forward to the end of the day, and the cider was already beginning to have an effect on him. But instructions were eventually at hand when the telephone rang, or would have been if Tommy had not proved so difficult.

The farmer answered the call which was from Mr King, who wanted to speak to Tommy. He had instructions to pass on as to which farm Tommy was to visit when he had finished where he was currently operating. The farmer went outside and called across to the field where Tommy and team were just winding up. 'Tommy, Mr King on the phone for you.'

'Tell him I can't come,' said Tommy. Well, the farmer was acting as piggy in the middle with Mr King declaring he had to speak to Tommy at one end and Tommy refusing to go to the phone at the other. Tommy suggested that the farmer should take the message and pass on the instructions or perhaps Mr King could speak to one of the crew. But his boss was adamant. He paid Tommy as a crew leader and it was only right he should speak to him. In the end, realising they were getting nowhere, the farmer relayed the message, much to Mr King's annoyance.

When the farmer had passed on the message, he told Tommy just how angry Mr King had sounded, and questioned if it was really worth it for Tommy to upset his employer in this way. Tommy replied, 'He might well 'ave been angry, but not 'alf zo angry as he'd abin if I'd 'ave answered thic vone and e'd a zmelt my breath!'

The shepherd and the magistrate

An old friend of mine and one time magistrate related how a veteran shepherd from the Quantock Hills was up before him in court one Thursday morning. Wednesday is market day in Bridgwater. It's the day the farming community bring their livestock to town and convert their animals into cash. On one such morning, the Quantock shepherd, having brought a flock of sheep to market, had realised a better price than expected.

The owner had told the shepherd that a percentage of the income from the sale was his and so he had something to celebrate. And that is just what he did, fortunately having banked most of the money first. Several pints of cider later, he was in such a state that he was unable to walk. Unluckily for him, his collapse took place right outside the front doors of the police station.

Within minutes he was safely tucked up in a cell. The following morning he was brought up in court, well hung over, faced with a prima facie case of drunk and disorderly behaviour, and the prisoner pleaded guilty. My friend fined the shepherd the smallest amount he felt he could impose – just £2.

With such a low penalty, it was with some surprise that the prisoner was heard to ask, 'Beggin' yer pard'n zir, but I don't get thic much money, zir. I woz wond'rin if you cin gi'e I time to pay?' Sympathetic to his plea, the magistrate declared he should pay the sum of 2s 6d each week for a period of 16 weeks until the debt was cleared.

The aged rustic, with both hands placed upon his shepherd's crook, replied, 'Thank 'ee, yer worship, but 'ow does I pay it?' The magistrate, now somewhat exasperated, explained how he should pay the instalments to the clerk of the court on a weekly basis until he cleared the debt. 'But tha's ridiculous, zir. 'Tiz only when I do come into town that I do git drunk. If I 'az to be yer every week vur zixteen weeks, then I'll never be out of yer debt, zir!'

And so arrangements were made for the fine to be paid through Merridge village post office.

Secret supplies

On a farm at Bishpool on the Quantock Hills lived a shepherd who was well known for his love of cider. He spent considerable time in the hills with the sheep, his main problem being how to keep a good supply of cider cool with so little shade available. But he had his own techniques, as the farmer's nephew discovered many years later. He was rabbiting one day when he had reason to put his hand down a rabbit hole. Instead of pulling out his ferret, out came a flagon bottle of cider! The shepherd had flagons stashed in rabbit holes all over the Quantock Hills, just like filling stations.

Welcome campers

A family of four very large characters were frequent visitors to the Home Farm caravan site at Burnham-on-Sea. A barbecue had been arranged and it seemed appropriate that sufficient local cider was available to wash down the hot dogs and burgers. And so one of the group went off to the Rich's Cider Farm where sufficient gallons were purchased to see the group through the evening.

Arriving back at the caravan site, the father of the group realised he needed somewhere cool to keep the cider. It was a strength-sapping, scorching hot day and so he placed the cider in the shade of the car boot sheltered in turn beneath the branches of a tree. It worked quite well. Father poured himself a glass and reclined in his chair, recovering from the exertion brought on by lugging around the containers of cider. It was not long before the glass was empty. Getting back onto his feet took some effort. This giant of a man was reclined well back into the low-slung sagging canvas. But another glass was poured and he reclined once more.

The time came for a third glass and the effort involved in extracting himself from the seat seemed to be increasing. Whatever the cause, these energy-wasting exercises would not do. A more sophisticated solution was required and the idea of a siphon appealed. So the cider container was raised to a higher level on the roof of the car and a length of plastic tubing inserted such that, by pinching the end, the cider would remain in the container but by releasing it, the cider would flow freely into the glass with the consumer never once leaving his seat.

It worked wonderfully. Father simply relaxed in his chair, slowly siphoning off the cider, quenching his thirst as the day became increasingly pleasant with the smell of the near complete barbecue wafting across from just behind his chair.

'Grub's up!' came the shout. The cider consumed had increased his appetite dramatically and he now rose from his recliner like a spring lamb newly born. But, like a new born lamb that has not yet found its legs, our camper had lost his. No sooner did he reach the vertical than his legs gave way and he collapsed in a heap, his head landing in the plates of food. Eventually staggering to his feet, it was clear to all present just how hungry he was – with a pork chop stuck to one ear and a bread roll to the other.

7

A Policeman's Lot

Penel Orlieu

Inevitably cider drinkers and officers of the law will come together but seldom in quite the way that one officer experienced during an encounter outside the Blue Boar Inn in Bridgwater. The Blue Boar is one of the many town centre pubs and is in an area called 'Penel Orlieu', a most unusual street name which requires some explanation.

Back in the times of the Normans, two of the many French families who found their way to Somerset were the Paynels and the Orlieus. Each had a street named after them. Where these two thoroughfares met was simply called Penel Orlieu.

But back to our police officer. He had just left the police station and was on his pedal cycle heading towards the town centre. Meanwhile, in the Blue Boar, a local cider drinker was well the worse for wear. Several pints of cider had left him barely able to stand. It was time to leave. He staggered across the bar, crashing into tables and spilling drinks as he did so, much to the annoyance of his fellow drinkers.

Now serious drinking men laugh at drunken behaviour, that is until someone starts spilling their drinks. And so the central character of our story met with a hostile reaction from the other customers and was consequently helped on his way home in such a way that he shot out of the door of the Blue

Boar Inn, barely touching the pavement as he rocketed towards the centre of the road.

Unfortunately this unexpected expulsion coincided with our police officer cycling by. The drunk went straight into the path of the local bobby who immediately shot over his handlebars and the drunk, the officer and the bicycle landed in a tangled heap.

Not without some struggling, the officer untangled himself from the mess, dragged the drunk to his feet and whilst holding him up by the collar, picked up his bike and escorted the drunk and the bike some fifty yards down the road into the High Street. There he leaned his bicycle against the wall of the Duke of Monmouth Inn, sat the drunk down on the kerb and took out his notebook. As he wrote, he explained to the drunk how he was being arrested for being drunk and disorderly and causing a police officer to fall off his bike. He read from his notes for the benefit of his prisoner stating that 'as I passed by the Duke of Monmouth, the accused shot out from the front door knocking me off my bicycle as he did so.'

'That's not true!' shouted the drunk. 'It's a bloody lie. It was outside of the Blue Boar.'

'Can you spell Penel Orlieu?' asked the officer. 'Course I bloody can't,' retorted the drunk. 'Well I can spell High Street,' replied the officer and continued with his arrest.

The new recruit

Occasionally it is a police officer himself who comes off the worst in relation to drink. But in this case, not for too many pints but for having his pint too full. Again this story relates to a Bridgwater officer, recently recruited and on one of his early tours of duty around the Eastover part of the town.

He had been made aware of an arrangement at one of the many pubs in the area where, if he went around to a side window at about ten o'clock at night, he would be given a pint by the friendly landlord. And so on his first night alone, he couldn't wait to take advantage of the offer. It was a cold, wet, miserable night and he needed cheering up.

On arriving at the pub, he walked around the side and tapped on the window. The landlord's head popped out and a pint was duly passed out to him. 'You're new,' said the landlord with his face displaying a huge smile, 'but more than welcome. Just stick the glass on the ledge when you've finished. Best of luck. Can't stop.' The head disappeared and the window closed.

One sip had been taken from the glass when our officer heard the sound of footsteps approaching around the corner. The footsteps had the familiar ring of another police officer. And there coming round the corner, just moments after our officer had tucked his almost full pint glass discreetly out of sight under his cape, was his sergeant. What was he to do? He just had to bluff his way out of this one and hope the sergeant moved on.

'Evening, lad,' said the sergeant. 'How's it going? All quiet?' he enquired.

'Oh, yes, sergeant,' replied our officer. 'Quiet as the grave.'

'Well, there's nothing going on at the station,' said the sergeant, 'so I thought I'd walk with you for a while. Come on, lad. Let's see if we can spot some crime. One quick arrest and we can get back to the station out of this drizzle.'

And so the two plodded their way around the new officer's beat with him all the while clutching his pint mug beneath his cape, cider continually slopping over the rim and seeping slowly down his uniform trousers. An hour or so had passed when the sergeant declared he'd seen enough. The town was quiet and in the safe hands of his new recruit. 'I'll go back to the station now, lad. Make sure you put the glass back before you finish!'

The devious sergeant had known all along and for an hour the officer had felt his pint splashing down his leg as they paced his beat. One final swallow and the glass was empty.

8

Cider Houses

Cider versus beer

As a lad I remember how the public houses in my home town were separated into cider houses and beer houses. The beer houses were simply referred to as pubs but a pub whose main income came from cider sales was derogatorily referred to as a cider house. I say derogatorily because these were viewed as the establishments frequented by the lowest classes, the drunks, alcoholics, unemployed and criminal fraternity. They were, of course, also frequented by those honest hard working folk who simply could not afford beer but still felt the need for occasional escapes from reality.

Cider was sold at a fraction of the price of beer and was considerably stronger. Those who needed to forget life's tribulations at the lowest possible cost would frequent the cider houses. They therefore had a spit and sawdust image and it was a rare occasion indeed when a lady would be seen in such an establishment unless she was the landlady or her daughter. They were also the premises where signs declaring 'No gypsies served here' were most likely to be seen, a practice which disappeared with the introduction of the Race Relations Act.

These were the premises to frequent if you wanted something that had fallen off the back of a lorry or if you simply wanted to enjoy good earthy conversation and talk about rabbits and ferreting. In my early twenties I used to visit one such pub when I walked my dog of an evening. The bar was the size of an average front room with wooden bench seats around three walls. Three heavy wooden tables stood in front of the bench seats completing the bar room furniture. Bare floor and bare walls were sufficient by way of decor. It was basic, it was crude but the company was good.

There were four or five of us who took our dogs there, something you would seldom see today when the sale of food is so critical to the survival of most establishments. The dogs, all well behaved, would curl up under the bench seat behind the legs of their masters while we discussed catching rabbits, market prices and what was wrong with the world today.

It was earthy but simplistic and with an honesty to it – nothing pretentious and nothing to prove. No one dressed up to go to the pub – they'd go straight from the fields on their way home and on the trip back from market. They were also exceedingly parochial. A stranger entering the bar would bring conversation to a complete standstill whilst the regulars quietly formed their private opinions of the incomer. These were not the pubs in which your besuited, tie-wearing businessman would be seen. But that was not the case in Bridgwater in the days leading to general elections.

Cider and politics

In Australia, there is a penalty imposed on all those who fail to vote in a general election. That means that those who vote are financially better off than those who do not. For centuries this was almost exactly how it was in Bridgwater. Everybody got paid to vote. There was no harm in it. It was still your democratic choice from which party you accepted the bribe, the Whigs or the Tories. And that was how Bridgwater people viewed the practice of voting.

59

Now those who had a vote were limited in number, perhaps four hundred in total. So there were not that many votes to buy. It was only the local business people who possessed the right to vote. These were the affluent few who would not be seen dead in a cider house, well beneath their stations. But the rules changed at election time for it was in the back room of the cider houses that payments for votes changed hands. Some cider houses were Whig houses, others Tory. So you could predict the outcome just by watching which houses the voters entered to accept their bribes. It was as obvious as pinning on a party rosette.

The corruption was publicly revealed in 1837, 1865 and again in 1868. A Royal Commission was set up to look into the voting practices in Bridgwater and its findings were that corruption was so much a part of the culture of the town that it would take several generations before Bridgwater could be trusted to vote fairly again. The town was disenfranchised at the end of the forty-seven day trial, and it was many years before any of the townsfolk were allowed to participate in general elections once more. Meanwhile, the cider houses slipped back to the practice of doing what they did best – selling cider.

Can cider influence the result of a riot trial?

In 1832 Bridgwater people rioted when the Tories declined to put up a candidate and hence there was no need for the Whigs to pay for any votes. Forty-three gentlemen were arrested and charged with causing a riot, an offence likely to lead to their deportation. The first six were sent to Taunton and their trial commenced but, thanks to their shrewd barrister, they got off on a technicality. The rest were sent to Wells since Taunton was no longer considered a venue where a guilty verdict could be achieved.

Due to the small size of the courtroom in Wells, the trial was held over two days. The accused, the jury, the judge and the witnesses were all obliged to share the same hotel overnight. Herein lay an opportunity for even more corruption. The Whigs put £500 behind the bar for the purposes of the entertainment of all those involved and to ensure all present could have a really good time. The beer and the cider flowed in abundance and the party continued through the night. Accused and jury alike found themselves sharing the same beds in the drunken confusion which ensued. Was it any wander that at the conclusion of the trial, each and every one of the accused were found not guilty?

With Bridgwater disenfranchised, we turn our attention to South Somerset. The 1885 elections appear to have been a period full of fear of riot. Candidates leaving the polling stations were stoned, returning officers were attacked and it was generally felt that it was safer to stay at home on polling day. But democracy must be seen to run its course and so the number of police on duty was increased in order to avoid any riotous behaviour. This proved particularly successful at Crewkerne where a high poll was recorded, no doubt thanks to the high numbers of county police who had their numbers swelled by some seventy special constables, sworn in especially for the occasion.

Indeed so thick were the police on the ground that the only trouble they had to deal with came from a group of special constables who became so drunk and unruly that they were disbanded in order to protect their fellow officers, with at least one officer being found in a completely drunken and unconscious state even before the polling stations had closed.

9

Carnivals and Cricket

The origin of the Somerset carnivals

Did you ever wonder how such a huge event as Bridgwater Carnival began, the largest illuminated carnival in the world from which have spun off those many other Somerset winter carnivals? And why are such popular events held so late in the year, long after the summer visitors have returned home? Well, perhaps we can blame that on the cider too.

Bridgwater once boasted the highest density of pubs per head of population of any town in the kingdom. In my early days there were one hundred pubs serving the needs of a population of twenty-two thousand inhabitants. So you can imagine the density of pubs in the town centre.

Traditionally Somerset had always been Protestant in its religious leaning and perhaps that explains the Duke of Monmouth's attraction to the town at the end of the 17th century. Perhaps it also explains why, at the beginning of that same century, Bridgwater's bonfire celebrating the failure of the Catholic Guy Fawkes to blow up a Protestant parliament was as lively and well supported as any in the country.

Those original bonfires served the purpose of burning the effigies of Guy Fawkes, or the Guys as they are now simplistically called. In the centre of Bridgwater, the various pubs around the Cornhill area made their Guys for the night of the bonfire and, when ready, brought them out to be revealed to the members of the public.

As the pubs paraded their effigies, the audience would offer their appreciation by way of applause. And by this method it was generally recognised which pub had produced the best Guy. There was no formal judging – just public reaction and common recognition. Being Bridgwater, it was never to stay that way for too long. Eventually someone broke with tradition and instead of producing a dressed dummy portraying Guy Fawkes, they brought out one in fancy dress.

The audience responded positively and to remain competitive the other pubs had to follow suit. And then the mould was broken again when a set of dummies was produced instead of just the one and as the competition increased, so did the number of dummies to a point where they needed to be carried on the back of farm carts. And then those who created the dummies dressed up to complete the illusion and sang and danced around the carts. So there we have it – the origins of Bridgwater Carnival.

Carnival camaraderie

Carnival today is part of the very life blood of Bridgwater and increasingly so across the county. Whilst the carnival clubs involved are extremely competitive, there is also a great camaraderie between them. That spirit is reflected in the way rival clubs bond together for such events as a weekend away in London. On one such occasion, the Ramblers, Vagabonds and Gremlins carnival clubs organised a combined weekend away, staying in the Regent Palace Hotel in the capital's centre. Being Somerset men, needless to say gallons of cider were taken with them in plastic containers. Their visit coincided with the Rugby League cup final being played at Wembley and hence the hotel also boasted a large contingent of northerners plus a contingent of Arabs.

When the Bridgwater lads gathered in one of the hotel bars, and began to consume their 'bring your own' cider, there appeared to be little for the hotel steward to do, and thus he closed the bar and left our friends to fend for themselves. When the Arabs and rugby supporters arrived, the usual Somerset hospitality was extended to them all and the cider flowed freely – at ten shillings for a plastic cup full.

With the rugby contingent was a particularly small man. Indeed he was so small that he could be seated in a small alcove in the wall where a vase might otherwise have been placed. And there, under the influence of the cider, he spent the rest of the night, drinking cider and singing for the entertainment of all.

Carnivalites sing at the drop of a hat and can keep the singing going for hours, with never a repeat to be heard. Against this background, the northerners and Arabs alike were soon under the influence of the golden liquid from Somerset. The laughter and singing could be heard deep into the hours of the morning, ably assisted by the world gurning (face pulling) champion who was also receiving his first lesson in the art of cider drinking. Those who knew him declared that never before had he pulled such faces and all to the sounds of 'Drink up thee zyder' in Yorkshire and Arab dialects. And to bring a perfect end to their weekend away, the contingent of carnivalites had just about covered the cost of that very memorable trip from their illicit sales of Somerset cider.

Somerset cricket and cider

A trip to London is remembered for similar reason by my good friend Stewart Richards. Stewart is a keen supporter of

Somerset cricket and in the days before it became necessary to tighten up security at the cricket grounds, Somerset supporters were famous for taking their cider with them. Indeed Gordon Rich of Rich's Cider was a regular watcher of cricket on the TV when Somerset were playing for he had an added interest. He used to see how many of his plastic containers he could count around the ground.

The better Somerset were doing in the competitions, the better were Mr Rich's sales. Open the back of a London-bound Somerset coach in the cricket season and it would be stacked high with containers of cider ready for the game.

It was on one such occasion that the Somerset supporters were sitting around the ground, intermingled with the rival Warwickshire fans with their cups of tea and glasses of squash. It was a friendly atmosphere in which, as Somerset batted, the West Country lads turned the conversation to their beloved cider. Cup after Warwickshire cup was upturned to empty out the tea and squash so the Midlanders could sample the contents of the plastic containers. They liked it, this innocuous yet refreshing beverage. They had one or two more – couldn't see what the fuss was about. It wasn't that strong. But before Warwickshire went in to bat, every last one of them was asleep. No verbal support came for Warwickshire that day!

Clive Lilley, a friend and distant cousin with whom I share the honour of having cycled from Land's End to John o' Groats, also remembers opposition supporters at another county game asking for a taste of the cider and offering their plastic vending beakers as receptacles. When filled with the cider, the plastic beakers went strangely and completely out of shape – as if the very beakers were drunk. Regardless of what this devil liquor was doing to the plastic, they drank it all the same and were grateful for the privilege.

10

Crime and Punishment

Punch drunk

There is an evil side to cider, as indeed there is with any form of alcohol. If it is taken in excess, rational behaviour is replaced by unexpected, often unacceptable conduct. Punch drunk is an expression with which we are all familiar. It is not a metaphor but an accurate description of that state of drunkenness in which the inflicted individual's demeanour becomes one of total aggression with a desire to punch anything and any excuse will do.

Perhaps the earliest record of such violent drunken behaviour is that which Robin Bush tells in his excellent book *Somerset Stories*. Therein he reveals how William le Faunt murdered Henry Beauflower in 1320 at the end of a night's drinking. Le Faunt had been drinking, and we must assume to excess, at the tavern of William Mere in Williton. On his way to his Carhampton home he passed through Stream, a hamlet within the parish of Williton, and there began an argument with Henry Beauflower. Such was the ferocity of the dispute that le Faunt took a bar from a door and with one blow to the head, felled and killed Beauflower.

William le Faunt disappeared and managed to evade punishment other than to have his worldly goods (a pig, a fishing net, a fish trap and a shelter) confiscated by the court

66

which tried him in his absence. The people of Williton were obliged to pay a halfpenny to the Crown as a deodand payment, a payment which dates back to mediaeval times where in the case of a murder, the value of the weapon must be paid as part of the forfeit. Since the door concerned belonged to the people of Williton, it was down to them to pay the forfeit.

Didn't know the gun was loaded

Many a pleasant evening has ended in disaster thanks to an excess of alcohol. Such was the case at the Rock House Inn on 20th May 1814[2]. The twenty-four year old James Pearce had sold his pamphlets and song sheets before calling in at the Rock House Inn near Curry Mallet. There he was joined by Thomas Burnell and the two men drank from eleven in the morning until eleven at night when the landlord advised them to take a bed at the inn.

On the brink of retiring, James Pearce was reminded by the landlord, James Hellard, that he still owed payment for two pots of cider. In a threatening manner, Pearce denied owing anything to the landlord who, imbued with the wisdom of many years' experience in the trade, decided to postpone the discussion until the morning when Pearce would be sober. But Pearce would not leave the matter alone and turned to violence. Hellard asked Burnell to restrain Pearce while he went to get the local constable. An hour and a half later he returned not with the constable but with a pair of handcuffs.

The attempt to apply the handcuffs brought about another violent outburst and Hellard took refuge behind the bar. Meanwhile Burnell fell asleep only to be rudely awoken by the sound of a shot from a gun. Pearce had taken a wildfowling

---

2 *Western Flying Post,* 22 and 29 August 1814; *Taunton Courier,* 26 May, 25 August and 1 September 1814

gun from off the wall and whether by accident or design had shot dead the landlord, leaving a widow with three children. At Pearce's four hour trial at the Wells Assizes for the wilful murder of James Hellard, the debate revolved around whether or not Pearce knew the gun was loaded and whether or not it had been half or fully cocked when taken off the wall. Had it simply gone off when he placed it on the table or had he cocked and fired it with intent to kill?

The jury found him guilty of murder and he was sentenced to death, but not before cider had once more played its part in the trial. One of the jury was found to be drunk during the trial and was arrested for contempt of court. Poor James Pearce never really stood a chance! His execution took place on 22nd August 1814.

Somerset's last public hanging at the crime scene

Kenn is a small village near Nailsea in the north of Somerset which gained notoriety in 1830 when the last public hangings at the scene of the crime in Somerset took place and the victims at the scaffold blamed their fate on the cider

William Wall was the thirty-five year old owner of a small cider house. Such houses were often the local centres for criminal activities with many a shady character lurking within their walls. The problem was that William Wall wasn't licensed and hence the drinking went on behind locked doors, which was fine as long as no one informed on the practice. But it

> *Then trust me, there's nothing like drinking*
> *So pleasant this side of the grave;*
> *It keeps the unhappy from thinking,*
> *And makes e'en the valiant more brave.*
> Charles Dibdin, Nothing Like Grog

only took one person to accuse a landlord in court for him to be found guilty. Since the authorities were keen to close down such establishments, it was not necessary to have a great deal of proof. Just one individual was needed as an informant.

Someone did just that and Wall was fined £20. He suspected that the informant was a local farmhand working for his neighbour Benjamin Poole. In revenge, Wall and his wife Mary persuaded two of their friends, thirty-two year old John Rowley and nineteen year old Richard Clarke, to burn down three stacks of wheat valued at £50 which belonged to Poole, a deed which was to attract the death sentence.

The act of arson was almost certainly intended as a warning to Benjamin Poole, a promise as to what would happen again should he ever inform on William Wall in the future. Perhaps it was equally intended to frighten off any other potential witnesses, for without an accuser there would be no trial. But these were the days when stealing a loaf of bread could result in deportation and the theft of such a simple item as a handkerchief could attract the death penalty. The law was not to be trifled with. A lesson had to be taught, not least because this instance of arson and intimidation was on the very doorsteps of the county's Chief Constable and High Sheriff, both of whom lived within a few miles of the crime. Perhaps therein lies the reason why the execution was held at the scene of the crime.

On 8th September 1830, the day of the execution, fifteen thousand spectators arrived to witness the event. It was considered to be a good day's entertainment and perhaps many of those present were aware of the changing mood towards public hangings and realised that this might be their last chance to witness such a public spectacle.

It's my opinion, sir, that this meeting is drunk.
Charles Dickens, Pickwick Papers

The execution party departed from Ilchester gaol at four in the morning on the forty-two mile journey to Kenn, the prisoners seated on their coffins as they travelled. At Axbridge they were met by the High Sheriff's javelin men in what we can presume to be a muscle flexing exercise to remind other would be villains not to mess on the High Sheriff's doorstep. At the village of Kenn itself they were joined by a hundred and fifty of the Chief Constable's men.

They arrived around midday to the sound of the funeral bell. The police officers formed a line along the route to ensure no interference from the expectant throng as the execution party processed from the Drum and Monkey public house. Prison governor, chaplain, High Sheriff, magistrates and local councillors formed the party of official dignitaries. Bringing up the rear was an open top wagon in which the prisoners stood in clear view of the now somewhat hostile crowd who hurled torrents of abuse at the three condemned men. Finally they were led to the scaffold. Rowley in a last desperate attempt to save his life put all the blame on Wall for having supplied the cider which led to his ruin.

At the roughly assembled gallows, in the seven acre field adjacent to that in which the stacks had been burned, the local vicar read a number of prayers to the kneeling prisoners. Across the gallows was a notice declaring 'For firing ricks'. As they rose to their feet, Wall pleaded with those assembled to forgive his wife who had also been sentenced to death along with Rowley's brother, but both had their sentences reduced to transportation.

Black hoods were pulled over the condemned men's heads. Their feet and hands were tied. Rowley pleaded to his family and friends to learn their lesson from his mistakes and Wall declared that he should have listened to his wife and never opened a cider house. The youngest of them all, Clarke, summed it up when he declared: 'Cider has been my ruin and the ruin of us all!'

'Cider … the ruin of us all!'

Standing in the back of the cart on which they arrived, they had the nooses placed around their necks, the horse's rump was slapped, the cart pulled forward and the three dropped to meet their maker. Rowley and Wall twitched momentarily as life extinguished. For poor Clarke, being younger and lighter, the executioner had misjudged the length of the drop required to effect a rapid death. He convulsed at the end of the rope until two of the execution party hung from his legs to hasten the end of his unnecessary suffering.

It was all over by lunchtime. The bodies were returned to Ilchester gaol for burial in an unmarked grave and Kenn slipped back into its rural routine. Mary, the wife of William Wall, was one of four others involved who had been found guilty at the same trial. But their punishment was deportation. For Mary this was preceded by thirteen months in prison where her eighth child was born. As to what happened to her other children we have no idea other than to assume that they would have gone into care within the local community.

> *They [pubs] make you as drunk as they can as soon as they can, and then turn nasty when they succeed.*
> Colin MacInnes, See You at Mabel's

Life or death on the toss of a coin

The Bell Inn in Bath was a popular watering hole for many of the city's coachmen in the early 19th century. It was kept by a lady known as Widow Roy, who lived there with her twenty-two year old errant son, James Taylor[3]. She did her best to keep a

---

3 *Sherborne and Yeovil Mercury*, 26th December 1808 and 17th April 1809; *Bath Journal*, 17th April 1809; also *Divine mercy as exemplified in the case of James Taylor who was executed at Taunton on the Tenth of April 1809 for the murder of John Dyer*, Philip Rose (1813) Bristol

warm and friendly establishment, with a good log fire burning in the parlour around which her coachmen clients would sit during the cold winter's nights.

Life could no doubt have been easier had it not been for her problem son James, a drinker, womaniser and gambler. He was a constant source of worry, drifting from one job to another with little sense of responsibility. He was arrogant and, when the liquor was in, aggressive. His hail fellow well met, warm and friendly greetings early in the evening could so easily turn to violence when the drink was in and the senses were out at the wrong end of a night's drinking. He was a man of two contrasting personalities and it was drink that determined which face he wore.

The widow did her best to teach him the trade, but he showed no inclination for work, far preferring to waste his time on idle pursuits in the company of his friends. His wayward lifestyle had, however, come to something of a climax and James had been obliged to marry Rebecca Rudman who was now carrying his child. Perhaps this new obligation would be just what he needed to recognise his social and family responsibilities. His mother hoped so and prayed this would be the making of him. The new year was approaching and with it the hope of a new start – but it was not to be.

It was three days to Christmas in 1808 when a group of mail coachmen arrived at the Bell Inn. Robert Johnson and Bill Guion had met in the afternoon and had decided to spend the evening at the Bell. The night was bitterly cold and the warmth of Widow Roy's parlour fire beckoned. There they were joined by John Dyer, a fellow coachman. Having ordered their food, they placed themselves before the fire and enjoyed the warmth as they downed their first cider of the evening.

Some while after, David Rice, a tailor, arrived with a lady friend. Courteously the coachmen invited the couple to join them around the welcoming flames of the burning logs. As the five sat and chatted, Widow Roy's son James arrived. With supper over, the more serious drinking was about to commence and James, with his usual extrovert style, demonstrated his strength by flattening spoons with his teeth.

Then the gaming began with the players tossing coins to see who should buy the next round. Unable to keep pace with the drinking, they shortly changed the stakes to cash; pennies to begin, then shillings as the inhibitions slipped away and finally guineas as the game inevitably slipped out of control.

The first guinea was played for and David Rice the tailor collected his winnings from the coachman Robert Johnson. No doubt looking to recoup his loss, Robert Johnson played and lost a second time. This was more than he expected, more than he could afford – foolhardy indeed! But foolishness in oneself does not enter one's considerations when alcohol replaces common sense and logic. He accused David Rice of foul play. What had begun as an entertaining diversion had now turned onto the path to tragedy, with the players about to act out the drama.

Rice was a moderate fellow and perhaps more sober and clearer thinking than the others. He realised the potential for the situation to become violent and offered a compromise. They would toss again. This they did and again Rice was seen to win fairly and he asked Dyer, who by now was the keeper of the stakes, to pass the winnings over. But once again Johnson cried foul and Dyer held onto the money.

Rice then demanded that James Taylor, as the son of the landlady, should act as independent arbitrator. Taylor declared Rice had won fair and square and the loser was requested to accept his financial loss. And that was the trigger for the violence which was to ensue.

Standing erect, Johnson called Taylor a liar. Taylor rose to the insult and in a fit of fury grabbed a chair and hurled it across the room. Stripping to his shirt, his anger was aimed at all present as he challenged them to take him on. There was no backing down now – no going back. With one sweep of his arm he cleared the table of all the glasses, expressing his contempt for those who failed to rise to his challenge. Then charging across the room like a raging bull, he crashed into Johnson, his accuser, and in a tumbling brawl pushed him into the passageway and from there they completed a rapid and painful descent down the stairs into the cellar.

The experience was sufficient to knock the wind out of the pair of them and, momentarily at least, common sense into their heads. Picking themselves up, there was a prospect of peace as the two men ascended the stairs with Taylor apologising for his behaviour and Johnson accepting.

Then Johnson realised a brooch of some sentimental value had disappeared from his coat and he demanded it should be searched for with no further delay. Taylor, perhaps keen to forget the night's affray, offered to search for it on the morrow and recompense for its loss if unsuccessful. But Johnson was obdurate. The search would begin now!

Bill Guion, perhaps in an attempt at peacemaking, offered to go with Taylor to the cellar and search for Johnson's missing item. This they did, and with success for the brooch was soon located. That, perhaps, thanks to Bill Guion's tactful assistance at the right time, could have been the end of the affair. But alas, as the two men ascended the stairs from the cellar, Guion, formerly the peacemaker, found it necessary to chastise Taylor for his unreasonable behaviour. This time it was Bill Guion who was attacked by Taylor.

Outside, the nightwatchman, William Roberts, had just called 'Past one o'clock' when he heard the noise of arguing coming from the Bell and slowly made his way in that direction. Also hearing the noise of the argument, Widow Roy entered the room where the fight was progressing and she wrestled the two men apart only for Guion to dash off into the taproom to grab a poker with which to defend himself whilst

Taylor, with his shirt torn from his back, retired to his room where his mother hoped he would find time to calm down.

The scene then unfolded very rapidly as Widow Roy, experienced from many years in the trade, realised peace would only be restored if she could keep her son in his room for long enough for her to evict the coachmen. Rushing to the top of the stairs she pleaded with her son not to come out until the coast was clear. She knew that the next time the protagonists met, events might prove to be beyond her control. Then rushing back downstairs on her way to evicting the coachmen she ran into Guion as he exited the taproom, poker in hand. Not stopping to think, he lay about her with the poker and her cries of 'Murder' were heard quite clearly by her son upstairs and by Roberts the nightwatchman who now sounded his rattle to summon further assistance as he hastened to the inn.

Throwing caution to the wind, Taylor opened a chest in his room from which he took two loaded pistols and ran downstairs to the rescue. Entering the taproom, he saw his mother cowering on a settee as Guion continued his attack with the poker. In defence of his mother, Taylor let fire one barrel. Guion was hit in the face and he fell to the floor declaring himself a dying man. John Dyer who had also been in the taproom was now running as rapidly as his legs would carry him towards the door leading out of the inn.

Temporarily blinded by the flash and stunned by the noise from his own pistol, Taylor spun around to be faced by the dark silhouette of a man immediately behind him. It was the nightwatchman who had just arrived and was entering the inn as rapidly as the barmaid was making her exit, closely followed by John Dyer.

Instinctively Taylor fired a shot in the direction of the threatening shadow, neither recognising nor hitting his target. In missing, he shot Dyer, the ball tearing his throat and neck. Leaving the nightwatchman no time to collect his thoughts, Taylor continued his attack, this time beating Roberts with his pistol handles until they broke. As he grabbed a poker to continue the assault, so fellow watchmen arrived on the scene and overpowered the raging villain.

The scene at the Bell was reminiscent of a battlefield. The beaten Widow Roy lay injured on the settee; Bill Guion lay with part of his face shot away; John Dyer, just the stake-holder in a game of toss, lay dying in a pool of blood.

Such was James Taylor's state of drunkenness, or perhaps such was his state of post traumatic stress, that he could later remember nothing of the events that had unfolded following his mother's cries of 'Murder'.

On Friday, 7th April 1809 at Taunton Crown Court, Baron Thompson presided over his trial. The verdict and sentence were predictable and on the following Monday, after the two mile ride in the back of a cart with spectators lining the route, twenty-two year old James Taylor faced his executioner at the Stone Gallows just outside Taunton.

Beneath the gallows the vicar joined him for final thoughts and prayers, leaving him to pray alone in his last moments. Rising to stand, he then looked around him for the friends who promised to be there at the end, and upon observing them, he acknowledged their presence with a small wave and turned his attention to the executioner.

The noose in place, he signalled his readiness to meet his maker by dropping a white handkerchief. The cart was drawn forward and the prisoner dropped. This normally would be the end of the story with the prisoner expiring after several moments of nervous twitching. Not so with James Taylor. No violent twitching as he entered his death throes but minutes of stillness at the end of which he raised his arms across his chest, as if entering a state of grace, and then expired. Four months later James Taylor Junior was born and baptised in St James's church in Bath.

A lucky escape

It was springtime in Yeovil in 1843 when the soldiers of the 67th Regiment of Foot visited the town on a recruitment campaign. Brightly dressed, they loudly boasted of their exploits. Whilst appropriate for the purposes of recruitment, such behaviour alienated the soldiers from many of the locals, for whom this was like a red rag to a bull.

A number of them were in the Running Horse Inn kept by Samuel Russell where a considerable volume of alcohol had been consumed[4]. No doubt their uniforms were provocation enough to Henry Phillips who, aggravated by their loud voices and boastfulness, found himself at the end of his tether. Assisted by several pints of cider, he challenged one of the more vociferous soldiers to a fight.

Prompted by the challenge, the soldier stripped to his waist ready to do battle. But no sooner were the two men ready to start than William Crocker, normally a quiet man and something of a gentle giant, stepped between the protagonists and declared there would be no fighting while he was there. And that perhaps would have been how the matter was settled had he not, somewhat unfortunately, continued by declaring himself to be the best fighter in the town. No self-respecting fighting man could ignore the challenge and one of the uniformed soldiers, George Watkins, suggested that he could prove William Crocker's boast to be unfounded. 'Then I will have a go at you,' he declared.

No sooner were these words spoken than the two men stripped off their respective jackets and retired to the outside yard followed by a band of spectators, including Crocker's wife. The two men took their positions and battle commenced. A

---

4 *Western Flying Post, Sherborne and Yeovil Mercury,* 15th April 1843; *Somerset County Gazette* 19th April 1843

fast and furious attack was launched. They fought several rounds with each going down in turn. Crocker, the stronger by far of the two men, got the upper hand and sent Watkins crashing back into a wall where a stone jutting out was positioned just right for Watkins' head to crash against it, rendering the soldier senseless and unable to stand.

In a fair fight, the soldier would at least have been allowed time to regain his feet, but this was drunken brawling and Crocker, grabbing Watkins by the shirt, raised him sufficiently to render a crashing backhander across the soldier's face leaving blood gushing from a cut under his eye and from his nose and mouth. Perhaps foolishly, Watkins staggered onto his feet only to be beaten down again and this time with Crocker's wife adding to the punishment as she set about doing even more damage with several blows to the back of his head. A third man also stripped to the waist, joined in with additional blows to Watkins' face.

In all mercy the soldier should not have been allowed to continue. But, finding his way back onto his feet, pride would not permit his surrender nor would chivalry stand in the way of Crocker continuing his punishment. At the request of Henry Phillips who had entered the inn, seconds were then appointed by mutual agreement but just in time the local constables arrived and stopped the proceedings.

Watkins was taken back into the pub to be treated for his injuries. Attempts to get some cider down him only appeared to make matters worse and any drink passing his lips was instantly vomited back up. Watkins spent the next few days at the inn and made a gradual but far from complete recovery. Sometime during the days after the fight, he had been walking the banks of the River Yeo when, having found an apparently convenient place to cross the river, and perhaps still weak from his injuries, he failed to complete his attempted leap from one bank to the next. Landing heavily, he rolled back into the icy waters of the river. Weak and cold, unstable and shaken, it took several minutes to extricate himself and it was one very sick-looking soldier who made his way back to his quarters.

It was not until sometime later that he sought the medical opinion of a doctor, Arnold Cole, who was passing by the Running Horse. The doctor looked at the feverishly shivering, battered and bruised wreck and ordered him straight back to bed where he was bled as part of the cure for the fever. For a few days he appeared to be slowly on the mend but then he took a turn for the worse with constant headaches. Despite daily visits from the doctor, within two weeks Watkins was dead. The coroner's verdict on the cause of death was the blows to the head compounded by the exposure to the cold.

Local witnesses to the fight described how they had seen the event unfold and how the fight was so uneven. Alfred Etheridge related how by peering though the gates he had seen Crocker and Watkins fighting whilst a third man also struck Watkins twice in the face. And so manslaughter was decided upon and Crocker was arrested in Crewkerne, to where he had fled. At Crocker's subsequent trial, the jury were left with the quandary as to whether or not Crocker was guilty of manslaughter. Were the injuries inflicted by him sufficient on their own to bring about Watkins' death? Had Samuel's blow been the fatal one? Was it the cold that killed him? Would he have survived had he not fallen into the river? Did the victim not bring it on himself by rising to the initial challenge when he could have walked away?

Mr Kinglake, defending Crocker, pointed out to the jury that unless they were certain beyond all doubt that Crocker's blows were the sole cause of death and that the other factors did not contribute to it, then they were bound to find him not guilty as charged. The evidence was such that they could not be certain, and he was found not guilty of manslaughter, and with that verdict avoided certain deportation for life. His six month gaol sentence for assault was a small price to pay and a sufficient period to reflect on the evil of an excess of alcohol. A newspaper report for the trial concluded: 'We cannot here refrain from noticing the many serious consequences which result from the existence of Beer Shops, and we are constantly in the habit of hearing of outrages and other disgraceful proceedings occurring at them which though happily not often attended by such serious consequences as in the present instance are nevertheless highly objectionable and deserving of general reprobation. These constant subjects of complaint and the manner in which these houses are abused call, we think, loudly for their suppression.'

'Brutal assault on the Police'

That was the newspaper headline after the trial of the killers of Police Constable William Penny[5]. In carrying out his duties, William Penny was beaten to death in yet another story where Yeovil's finest were obliged to deal with the drunken behaviour of its ill behaved minority.

It was January 1862 and fifteen or so navvies had been quaffing cider in the Railway Inn at the bottom of Hendford Hill after their day's work. As they eventually walked homeward bound, noisy and boisterous, they passed Constable William Hubbard who bid them a goodnight. Their response was mixed but amongst the replies Hubbard could clearly hear abuse aimed directly at him. These were hard, tough men and Hubbard erred on the side of caution and ignored the taunts and the deliberate barging he received as he passed George Hansford.

---

5 *Western Flying Post*, Yeovil, 28th January 1862

81

He was not far past the group when the sound of crashing stones immediately behind him added to his unease. Turning, he saw Hansford aim a stone in his direction, but it was well wide of its target, as were other missiles which followed. Now it is important to realise that up to now, no one had been hurt. The behaviour of the drunks constituted a misdemeanour, for which the culprits could be arrested subject to a magistrate's warrant being issued. It was not an arrestable offence as such in the absence of a warrant.

Discretion being the better part of valour, Hubbard made his way up the hill away from the hostile mob to where he knew Constable Penny, a well liked and respected local policeman, would be waiting. Penny, on hearing of the incident, was determined to arrest at least one of the culprits and together the two officers went in pursuit of the gang of navvies.

When Constable Hubbard identified Hansford, Penny entered the group, announcing Hansford's arrest. When Hansford refused to go it appeared that all hell was about to break loose and Hubbard, still cautious, called Penny back declaring they would go for reinforcements. As it happened, Sergeant Keats, having heard the commotion, was already on his way and soon the three officers caught up with the navvies at the Red House Inn. An immediate attempt to arrest Hansford was sufficient to trigger a violent reaction from at least three of the navvies although most of the group dispersed, wishing to play no further part in the fracas.

George Chant and Charles Rogers joined the affray with club-sized sticks and punches flying everywhere. Penny and Keats were knocked to the ground as Rogers wielded his club. Hubbard took its full force in his face just before Rogers turned and fled, leaving behind a scene of carnage. Hubbard recovered sufficiently to go in pursuit and the full force of his anger was unleashed on the now exhausted Rogers who was arrested. Back at the original scene, the collapsed body of William Penny was still coming under attack from the other two assailants. Keats came to the rescue and arrested Hansford whilst Chant managed to effect his escape.

The fighting over, the severity of Penny's injuries became apparent and the officers carried their badly beaten colleague into the inn where he was nursed by the landlady, Mrs Rendall, for the next few days. Hubbard rushed into Yeovil for medical assistance, allowing Rogers to escape.

An initial improvement, during which Penny was taken home, was not to last for long and within six days of the fight, William Penny died from his wounds in his West Coker home. One by one those responsible for his death were arrested and eventually brought to trial. When Charles Rogers was discovered in hiding in Dorchester and arrested, he told the arresting officer, 'If I hadn't hit 'e, e'd a killed I.' All were charged with murder and all pleaded not guilty to the crime which would bring an automatic death penalty if proven.

The trial commenced on the last day of March 1862 and what a successful defence solicitor Mr Ffooks turned out to be acting on the prisoners' behalf. The case he argued was that the original offence of stone throwing was a misdemeanour and not an offence for which an arrest was permitted without a magistrate's warrant. Therefore the arrest was unlawful and the three accused were entitled to resist it. Indeed it was the officers themselves who were at fault and it was they who should stand accused, he declared.

His argument won the day. Two of the offenders were acquitted and Hansford was found guilty of manslaughter by the jury with a recommendation for mercy. But the judge took a less lenient view and Hansford was sentenced to four years imprisonment. William Penny was laid to rest in his village churchyard at West Coker where his headstone records his untimely demise.

The policeman and the poachers

As we have seen, cider related violence was commonplace around the middle of the 19th century. In 1843 we had the trouble at the Running Horse, then Constable Penny after his violent death was buried in the graveyard at West Coker. But nearby East Coker was to add its name to the list of cider induced murders just a few years later.

It was 1876 when another policeman was murdered, not this time, as far as we can tell, by the violent act of drunken villains, but apparently by a quite sober gang of poachers. The subtle twist in this case was that it was the police officer who perhaps had taken one too many and, as a result of that, his judgement had been somewhat impaired.

There was a more relaxed attitude to drinking on duty in the 19th century, for example in the case of agricultural workers and those on long voyages. But my next story took place in November, not the time of year when a thirst needed to be quenched by several pints in the course of a day's activity.

The village policeman was Nathaniel Cox, a popular, well liked individual who enjoyed his drop of cider. He was a well built, thirty-seven year old, a confident character and a father of four children. On the tragic evening when Cox was to lose his life in the line of duty, he joined fellow officer Henry Stacey at the White Post Inn. After several drinks they left the pub around ten o'clock and headed off towards Netherton, their way illuminated by their regulation issue lanterns.

The following day the nearby Yeovil Fair was to take place and both officers knew this major event in the local social calendar would attract a great number of cheapjacks, conmen, pickpockets and other shady characters. They also knew that with the police activity focusing on the fair and with members of the public being drawn to the event leaving their homes unattended, burglars and poachers alike would take advantage of the situation. So a careful eye would be kept for unscrupulous looking strangers. The first hint of such characters on the loose came when the two officers passed a horse and cart with three men seated and perhaps a fourth in the back. A polite exchange of 'good evenings' was all that passed between the officers and possible villains.

An hour or two later, the officers were at the home of Farmer Squibb near the road where the horse and cart had passed. If the characters on board were out for a bit of poaching, then they would probably pass back the same way with the load of ill gotten gains on board. Awaiting their return was pleasant enough when the farmer was keeping the officers supplied with pints of cider.

After several pints at the White Post Inn and yet more at the farm, we have to question whether or not the officers were in full control of their faculties when they went out to challenge the returning band? Cox seized the reins of the horse and demanded to be shown the contents of the cart. A rapid exchange of arguments was followed by a rapid exchange of blows at the end of which Cox lay at the side of the road with his brains protruding through his skull, his crushed helmet lying nearby. Stacey, momentarily unconscious, lay face down in a ditch, his head and body covered in cuts and bruises from blows from clubs and boots, sufficient to render him senseless.

When he regained his feet in the darkness, there was no sign of his colleague. In the distance was the dim light of a farm to which he staggered, drifting in and out of consciousness. Hammering on the door brought the farmer's attention and he, having grasped some understanding of what had happened from Stacey, aroused two of his labourers and the group set off to attempt to find Constable Cox. Just a matter of yards from where the fracas took place, Cox's body was discovered.

In the weeks that followed, the four men involved were rounded up, all being well known local villains. At the trial, the quantity of cider consumed by Cox and Stacey came into question. Stacey said how they had partaken of one or two drinks, but nothing excessive. Apart from the White Post Inn and the farm, where we know several pints were consumed at one and yet more at the other, it seems they also visited the Red House Inn at Stoford where they had a drink or two, and likewise at a private house before they settled down with Farmer Squibb. So it was rather surprising that PC Stacey should consider that when the two of them left the farm just moments before the ill fated episode, they were both quite sober!

On the final day of the trial, the courtroom was packed and there was quite unruly behaviour from members of the public horrified by the death of their local and popular constable. Poachers and sheep stealers were also there, perhaps to witness the potential punishment should they be captured themselves for similar crimes.

Throughout the trial the defence solicitor played on the amount of beer and cider the two officers had consumed. He pointed out how Cox had overstepped his authority in stopping the cart with no proof of any crime being committed. He stressed how the defendants were entitled to protect themselves when challenged unlawfully. But he knew the mood of the court was against the accused and different tactics would be required to succeed in keeping his clients from the hangman.

The defence argument, just prior to the jury withdrawing to make their decision, had been based on the fact that whilst the officer had undoubtedly been murdered, the jury had to decide who was responsible. Had all four been guilty of murder or just some of them? Unless they were absolutely confident in their own minds that they knew exactly who murdered the officer, then there were no grounds to find any one of them guilty.

To the surprise of all present, the jury returned a verdict of not guilty of murder but guilty of the lesser charge of manslaughter for each of the four. The judge showed mercy in the case of the eldest defendant, his view being that he was not as involved as the others, and granted him a free pardon. Each of the other three was given twenty-four years imprisonment.

In the graveyard in East Coker the headstone marking the last resting place of Nathaniel Cox can still be seen today.

Daughter slaughtered for the price of cider

Perhaps one of the saddest of all the stories where cider led to the ruination of a family comes from Simonsbath on Exmoor. It is particularly distressing since it involves the killing of a young innocent girl, murdered by her father who preferred to spend money on his cider habit rather than the keep for his daughter.

William Burgess was not a pleasant man. He was dishonest, a swindler, sheep stealer and alcoholic. His wife had died and left him with three children at their cottage home alongside the White Water stream. But Burgess' mind was not set on the welfare of his children, only his drinking. He was first and foremost a conman and travelled the area acquiring money from well intended, well to do folk who fell victim to his hard luck stories – mostly of a contrived nature, tugging at the very heartstrings of his victims.

With the money he came by, he embarked on drinking binges lasting days at a time. Against such a background, his children were a considerable inconvenience. He placed the two older ones into service, but young Anna was left in his care, not old enough yet to work. Burgess and Anna moved into Gallon House Cot, a cottage conveniently next to the Gallon House Inn. But Anna was costing two shillings and sixpence a week to keep and, at his trial, Burgess gave that as the reason

87

why he had to kill her. She was a drain on his cider drinking resources. Having brutally murdered his daughter, he took her body and buried it in the side of a bank up on the moor.

Now sheep stealers would do just this when they had rustled and killed a sheep. They would place it in a shallow grave to be collected later. Unfortunately for Burgess, two of his sheep stealing friends had witnessed the burial but not recognised the character they saw as him. They explained to him later that day how they had seen someone, well off in the distance, apparently burying a sheep – and on their patch. Now they knew that Burgess would have told them had he taken a sheep so it never occurred to them that the stranger in the distance was Burgess himself, nor that he had murdered young Anna.

Shattered by what his fellow felons had seen, that night Burgess went up onto the moor and recovered his daughter's body. He carried her to the disused Wheal Eliza Mine, which had been closed for many years and was now deeply flooded. There he dropped her down the long shaft.

Some days later the burnt remnants of Anna's clothes were found around the back of his cottage. Questions as to her whereabouts received the response that she had gone to stay with her grandmother in Porlock. Further enquiries proved this to be untrue and shortly afterwards Burgess disappeared. It was suspected that he had gone to South Wales via Lynmouth and it was indeed in South Wales that he was captured and from whence he was returned to Dulverton, and then to his trial at Taunton.

But first a body was required if murder was to be proven. Throughout the summer and autumn, parties searched the moors for signs of a grave. Nothing could be found. But in time Burgess's two sheep stealing companions had come to the conclusion that the man they had seen, apparently burying a sheep, had probably been Burgess himself burying his daughter. And the dark figure they had seen later dropping something into the mine shaft, after they had mentioned their sighting to Burgess, had probably been Burgess once again.

Under a cloak of confidentiality, they told the local vicar of their observations and he in turn notified the authorities. The judge ordered that the mine shaft should be pumped dry. It took many weeks but the result was the discovery of Anna's body. It was five months since her death and her face was now unrecognisable. She was identified by her hair alone. Already buried twice, Anna's little body was taken away for a Christian burial to her third and final resting place. Her father was found guilty of her murder.

On 4th January 1859 William Burgess was executed by hanging in full public view. Young Anna is now safely laid to rest, the victim of her father's cider drinking addiction.

11

Drinking and Driving

The rebel and the ditch

It's hard to believe when we look back just how common drinking and driving was before the introduction of the drink drive laws. It was rampant and I could tell of many stories of excess. Near my own home is the Halfway Inn on the road from Bridgwater to Westonzoyland. A good deal of cider used to be sold there but less so these days. One of the characters who was a regular at the Halfway was a chap called Jack Symonds. He lived in the nearby hamlet of Dunwear. Jack was well known for the large volume of cider he consumed.

I can reflect back to an autumn evening when I was cycling past the Halfway Inn on my way home. It's a story related in my publication *Somerset Stories of the Supernatural* but it is equally at home within these pages. I visited a friend, Tim, at Fowler's Plot, on the edge of Chedzoy and close to the Sedgemoor battlefield area. I was courting at the time and my fiancée, now my wife Lorna, was with me, as was a lifelong friend, later to be our best man.

As we departed, Tim warned us to beware of the ghost of a rebel who haunted the junction of the country road along which we were about to cycle and the main road between Westonzoyland and Bridgwater. He described how the rebel could be seen in the ditch at the junction, just the top half of his body visible. This unusual behaviour was explained by Tim who described how the old road had been much lower than that of today, and some yards over from its present line. The rebel was simply walking the old route.

We left Tim, not taking his comments seriously but with the seeds of doubt already sown in each of our minds. As we slowed on approaching the haunted junction, our dynamo bicycle lights dimmed. We checked we were safe from oncoming traffic and crossed the road, turning right as we pointed ourselves towards Bridgwater. And as our lights picked up in intensity and swept across the line of the ditch, there before us, as real as life, was the top half of a man projecting from the ditch just as described by Tim.

Lorna had never cycled so fast before – nor indeed has she matched her speed since – that incident. We eventually caught up with her back in Bridgwater after a delay of ten minutes or so. This was no ghost we had seen but Jack Symonds, to whom I referred earlier, a local man who enjoyed a drop or two of cider in the nearby Halfway Inn.

In fact Jack went well beyond a drop or two on most evenings and on many occasions failed to complete the wobbly cycle ride to his Dunwear home without ending up in one of the ditches which inconveniently lined both sides of his route. This particular evening he had travelled little more than a few hundred yards before meeting his demise.

Such was the regularity of Jack's falls from his bike that he carried a virtually permanent gravel rash on his face but his appearance wasn't sufficient to stop him getting employment for a while at the Hinkley Point Nuclear Power Station. There he would arrive at six forty-five in the morning, already looking as though he had a head start on the cider jar. One of his fellow employees told me how in his flask he would carry cider despite the total ban of alcohol on the site. Fortunately for the residents of Somerset, the power station survived its encounter with Jack.

Egg and chips

Sadly Jack passed away some years ago and there is little doubt that cider hastened his demise. But in his day Jack was a character, as so many cider drinkers were. My old friend Duncan Smith remembers how as an eighteen year old, left in charge of the Halfway Inn while the licensees were away, he was asked by Jack for a pint of cider and some egg and chips.

The pint duly served, Duncan retired to the kitchen from which he later returned carrying a plate of egg and chips which he proudly placed in front of Jack, this being the first such meal he had prepared. 'What d'ya call that?' asked Jack, not looking at all amused. 'Egg and chips!' retorted Duncan. 'That's not what I want,' responded Jack. 'I want a packet of crisps and a pickled egg!'

Duncan's grandfather was another regular at the Halfway and a keen cider drinker. On one occasion, after four pints of Natural Dry, or Natch as it is colloquially known, he jumped in his car, drove out of the car park and straight across the road into the ditch opposite. Natch had that effect on people and if there were no other reason for introducing the drink drive laws, at least they are there to protect us against the consequences of Natch. A few other nice Bridgwater related stories come to mind. One of the railways, three of the open road and one of the river.

Not drunk is he who from the floor
Can rise alone, and still drink more;
But drunk is he, who prostrate lies,
Without the power to drink or rise ...
T. L. Peacock, The Misfortunes of Elphin

The runaway train

Bridgwater could once boast two railway stations, one being the Bristol to Exeter or the old Great Western, and the other the Somerset and Dorset line. On the S & D it was the guardsman's habit when the train pulled into Bridgwater station to take the short walk down to the Cross Rifles Inn where he would partake of a pint or two before the train recommenced its journey back up to the main line.

On one such occasion, as he sat quaffing a jar, the porter helped to load the goods van at one end of the train whilst the driver and stoker attended to the engine at the other. It was a cold frosty evening in which the steam from the engine lingered low along the full length of the platform making visibility somewhat difficult.

Peering through the steam, the engine driver waved his hand from the cab requesting the signalled response from the guardsman that it was safe to pull out of the station. Perhaps the cider was particularly fine that day for the guardsman was still in the Cross Rifles. However, the newly recruited porter was there at the other end of the platform and not wishing to cause offence so early in his career, on seeing the engine driver's wave, politely waved back.

Through the mist the driver mistook the identity of the person waving as his guardsman. The explosive sound of steam escaping sounded as the brakes were released and with a slow and deliberate chug-chug the engine switched into gear and pulled its load away from the platform.

Back in the Cross Rifles it was with total disbelief that the guardsman listened to what sounded incredibly like his engine leaving without him. Rushing to the door of the inn, his worst fears were confirmed. Thanks to his love of cider, there went his train. How would he explain this one to the boss?

Horse-drawn days

I'm sure there would never have been the need for drink driving laws if only we had stuck to horse-drawn travel and Shanks's pony. No matter how busy the roads became, there was something very safe about a horse and cart. In fact, the drunker the driver, the better. Let me explain. A sober driver is a problem to no one. Nor is one who is totally drunk. Throw the drunken owner in the back of the cart and a well practised horse will gently plod its way home none the wiser as to the state of its owner.

Such was the case at John Sparkes' grandfather's farm at Perry Green. John had cousins who lived over the border in Devon. Each year they would visit Bridgwater's St Matthew's Fair at the end of September and then spend the night at their teetotal grandfather's at Perry Green. They would arrive each year in a pony and trap. One year they stayed too long in the beer tent knocking back the cider. Granddad awaited their arrival but to no avail and off to bed he went.

Then at three in the morning he was awakened by the sound of a horse's hooves on the stones outside the farmhouse. Lighting a lantern, he went out into the dark to find the horse and an apparently empty pony trap waiting in the yard. There being no signs of life, he began to wonder what disaster could have befallen his family. The horse was fine and the trap seemed to be in order. Indeed it was so tidy, the tarpaulin cover to keep out the rain when not in use was neatly fixed in place over the top of the trap.

Something made Granddad lift the tarpaulin and look beneath. There, under the cover, and unconscious to the world, were all the members of his family, each in an oblivious state of slumber. The amazing aspect of this story was that the horse only made that trip once a year, that is from the other side of Wellington to Bridgwater Fair and from there to Perry

Green. How amazing that the horse should remember where to go. But then, like Granddad, he was teetotal too.

It's the in between stage of drunkenness that is the most dangerous, not the state where the driver is totally drunk, nor totally sober, but where the driver is drunk but doesn't yet know it. Then he is a threat to his own safety and that of others. But in days of yore an early form of wheel clamp could often provide a solution to their problem! There was a common practical joke which was played especially on strangers discovering the effects of cider for the first time. Once again an example comes from John Sparkes. His grandmother's family farmed at Stogursey and there one day Tommy Chidgey arrived with a horse-drawn load of coal. Having delivered the half ton load, he went to the cider shed for the customary glass of farmhouse cider. The trouble was he stayed too long and really wasn't in a fit state to drive the horse and cart home. But whilst he was imbibing, someone else unhitched his horse from its traces, repositioning the horse and cart so that the horse was on one side of a wooden fence rail and the cart on the other. The two were then reconnected with the fence rails in between and left to await the drunken owner's return.

In another old story of horse sense, a character by the name of Lucky Day from North Petherton used to complete the weekly journey from his home to Bridgwater's Wednesday morning market. This he did in his horse and trap. Lucky being partial to a drop of cider, the horse knew every public house between the market and his home.

Apparently one night the horse on its homeward journey stopped outside the George, but Lucky never dismounted to take his usual pint or two. When the landlord went out to see what was keeping him from entering the bar, he discovered that Lucky was dead where he sat with the reins still in his hands. The landlord simply slapped the horse's rump, sent him on his way and returned to his customers. You can imagine how he announced the news when the regulars asked if Lucky was coming in or not – 'No, not tonight. He's gone on 'ome 'cos he's dead!'

Jibo Searle, river pilot

Jibo Searle was a river pilot of exceptional ability. He was the captain of the *Crowpill*, a coal carrying boat for the Sully Coal Company in Bridgwater and in that role he regularly sailed between South Wales and Bridgwater, navigating the treacherous River Parrett on a daily basis. No one knew the river like Jibo and his knowledge of the changing sandbanks and channels never ceased to amaze the locals as out of the densest of fogs would appear the *Crowpill* with Jibo at her helm. Yet with such an instinctive ability, it was even more amazing that at certain times of the day his navigational skills would completely desert him.

These strange occurrences always manifested themselves when it was approaching closing time at the quayside pubs at Bridgwater. As Jibo rounded the bend in the river approaching the Dunball wharf where the Greenfield Arms served the mariners and road travellers alike, he would look at his watch, consider the few miles still to go, contemplate the tide and visibility, and then declare it unsafe to proceed any further that evening!

Waterside cider houses

Cider houses were very much part of the Somerset based sailors' way of life. Not only were the dock areas around Bridgwater and Watchet densely populated with such houses, but the same applied along the length of our canals. Once the ships arrived at Bridgwater, where they moored up either in the dock or along the River Parrett's quaysides, their goods were unloaded and for the most part trans-shipped onto barges for onward passage into the Somerset hinterland, destined for Langport or Taunton and beyond.

Much of the loading of cargo onto the barges was done by hand, and likewise the unloading at the end of the journey. In between the barges had to be navigated to their destination, either towed by horse along the canal or using the tide to take them up the river. Either way it was hard physical work. And so, alongside the river, there were watering holes, cider houses such as the Thatchers Arms at Moorland, the King Alfred at Burrowbridge and the Black Smock at Staithe. Then there were the canal pubs like the Boat and Anchor at Huntworth, the Harvest Moon at North Newton and the Bathpool Inn.

In addition, many farms along those routes would have their cider rooms and here the boatmen could stop off for refreshments or a bed for the night. In return, the farmer attracted to his premises men who brought with them goods that were less conveniently moved by road. And for many of these low lying establishments, the boats were the only practical form of transport during the winter floods.

In summer it was in these cider rooms that not only the boatmen would gather, but the farm labourers as well. And so there was a fascinating mingling of farm labourers who rarely left the farm and boatmen who were rarely in the same place two nights in a row. Since most could neither read nor write, these cider rooms became little Rialtos where the whole local community could listen to news from the outside world, news which undoubtedly became increasingly exaggerated as the cider intake increased.

Dad's Army

In issues of drinking and driving, it isn't always the driver who is responsible for injuries caused by the drunken state, as one member of Cranmore's Dad's Army discovered to his great discomfort. Donald Brown, in his publication *Somerset v Hitler* which deals with secret wartime operations on the Mendips, tells how members of the Cranmore-based unit of the Land Defence Volunteers were required to go and inspect the Wedmore unit.

Unfortunately they called at an inconvenient moment when one of the Wedmore group had to disappear to do the milking. It was just as well the Germans weren't attacking at the time! And so to overcome the problem, it was agreed that one of his fellow Wedmore men would take the Cranmore crew down to the New Inn. Now the arrangement was that they should be kept in the inn for as long as it took to complete the milking and for the man concerned to return to his post, his absence unnoticed.

Well, the cider was particularly good and the Cranmore men never quite got around to completing their mission. In fact, so much time had been spent in the inn that, by the time they had to return, one of their unit was almost out for the count. He was virtually poured into the back seat of their army vehicle and the door slammed behind him. So well anaesthetised was he that it was only when they tried to get him out at Cranmore that they realised his fingers had been shut in the door for the complete length of the journey.

Another wartime experience comes from John Sparkes whose father, whilst teetotal himself, kept ample cider on his Chilton Polden farm for the labourers. This being wartime, there were a number of Royal Engineers billeted nearby and they provided a useful source of additional labour at harvest time. After an evening in the field, they would return to the farm to share the cider set aside for their use.

However, on one such evening, John and his father, who had been milking in the late afternoon down in the fields at Gold Corner, took longer than expected and were late in returning to get the soldiers started on the harvesting. The soldiers, not ones to miss an opportunity, decided that to save time later they would let themselves into the cider barn and have their cider ration before starting the harvesting. By the time John and his father arrived it was already too late. They were all blotto and from that day forth the cider barn was kept safely padlocked.

Spies in their eyes

One of the effects of wartime propaganda is that any stranger to a town is liable to be treated with suspicion and perhaps deemed to be a spy[6]. Such was the case in August 1914 when Lieutenant Palmer of the London Scottish Rifles stopped at the Hare and Hounds in Shepton Mallet on his way to rejoin his regiment after a period of illness. There he was unfortunate enough to make the acquaintance of Rupert Morford, the local vet. Now Rupert had imbibed a cider or two to the extent that he was in a moderate state of drunkenness, sufficient that he could hold a conversation but not come to sensible conclusions.

Rupert, having espied the uniformed gentleman and not recognising the uniform, inferred incorrectly that the man was a spy. Assuming the role of Spycatcher General, he offered the officer a drink and entered into conversation. This turned to interrogation much to the amusement of the officer as he watched this recent acquaintance furiously scribbling details in his notebook like a demented detective. The amusement turned to annoyance when on making his move to leave, the officer was 'arrested' by Morford who ordered him to put his hands up declaring he had enough evidence in his notebook to hang him as a spy.

---

6 *Western Gazette*, 21st August 1914

Morford's declarations were so loud as to attract a crowd and they were soon persuaded that there was a spy in their midst, such was Morford's conviction. The arrival of two police officers saved the day as they realised the innocence of the officer and the drunken state of Morford. Told to go home, Morford became somewhat violent, no doubt convinced by now that the police officers must be part of the same spy ring. Fists flew and Morford had to be restrained. The gathering crowd, now fed by rumour rather than fact, were hell bent on the downfall of the 'spy' and Morford and Palmer both had to be taken to the police station for their own safety.

Morford continued to be a nuisance. An attempt to release him once more resulted in him whipping up the crowd into a frenzy which resulted in Morford being locked up for the night and the army officer's car being vandalised and its tyres slashed. Eventually, with the car repaired at the local garage, Palmer slipped out of the town sometime after midnight, once the rioters had gone to their beds. Morford, the normally respectable veterinary surgeon, was brought up before the magistrates the following day and found guilty of drunk and disorderly behaviour.

I've taken more out of alcohol than alcohol has taken out of me!
Winston Churchill

12

Men Behaving Badly

Punkies and drunks

There's no escaping it, when the cider's in the senses are out and there are countless instances of the gentlemen in particular being less than gracious in their drunken stupor. One such example comes from Hinton St George in South Somerset where Punkie Night is still celebrated as a reminder of just how pathetic mass drunkenness can be. Legend has it that the Hinton men went one night to the nearby Chiselborough fair and took with them all the lanterns so that they could find their way home. But at the fair they partook of an excess of cider and spent many happy hours chatting to the young Chiselborough ladies. Back in their home village, the ladies began to worry and set off in search of their menfolk.

Now without the benefit of lanterns, all they could do was to hollow out mangel-wurzels, a large kind of beet, in the fashion of Hallowe'en pumpkins. With these as lanterns, they trekked across the hill to the nearby village to retrieve their husbands and lovers. The men, seeing the glowing lights approaching from across the hill and coming from the direction of their own village, thought that evil spirits had been visiting their loved ones in their absence. Such was their inability to focus on the approaching throng and so far were their senses of logic diminished by the excess of cider that the reality of the situation failed to dawn on them.

Fearing the worst, there was an immediate rush to get home, but not by the way they had come. Now men usually find Dutch courage when the drink is in and are often prepared to take on all comers in an exaggerated belief in their own prowess. But that is the case when dealing with the familiar. When confronting the unexpected and inexplicable, all such macho bravado goes out the window. The Hinton revellers erred on the side of safety and took the long way home, avoiding the evil spirits and conveniently giving the wives, who had realised what was happening, plenty of time to return to their home village ahead of their menfolk.

The women never let them forget that night and each year the young children of the village walk in procession through the streets of the village with their punkie lanterns held high as they sing their punkie song.

It's Punkie Night tonight, It's Punkie Night tonight
Give us a candle, give us a light, It's Punkie Night tonight
It's Punkie Night tonight, It's Punkie Night tonight
Adam and Eve wouldn't believe, It's Punkie Night tonight

And talking of Adam, it's interesting to contemplate the Somerset theory that had the Garden of Eden been in Somerset, Adam would probably have turned the apple into cider rather than taking a bite. And then what would have happened to the human race?

Sold his wife at the fair

When a married couple are childless for long enough it is often the case that doubts begin to creep in as to which of the couple is unable to produce the longed for child. Perhaps that

Poor Betty Bodger!

was the case with John and Betty Bodger[7]. Married for some years, Betty had failed to produce any offspring and John, for whatever reason, decided to take her to the fair, and I suspect it was Bridgwater Fair in 1761, and auction her.

7 Somerset Record Office DD/TB wife contract 1761

Imagine Betty's trepidation as they headed to the fair ground. What kind of a man would sell his wife in this way, and what kind of a man would buy one? Betty could have been going from the frying pan into the fire. But it appears to have been with her consent since the document recording the sale has the mark of all three characters involved, John Bodger, Betty and James Bacon, a fisherman of Stogursey who was the other party in the transaction. It was James who bought her for the sum of £5.

Well, James and Betty went to James' Stogursey home and there they settled down together. Within two years they were married in Stogursey church, presumably suggesting that the Church of England recognised selling one's wife at the fair as a legal form of divorce. About a year later comes the registration of the birth of a daughter, the first of seven children.

Have you remembered the reason John sold Betty? Because of her apparent infertility. So who was to blame in the Bodger household? Perhaps we can blame it on the cider!

The errant Billy Bacon

Cider was certainly to blame in the marriage of young William Bacon[8]. It was 1748 when this eighteen year old lad from Sampford Arundel was working as a labourer at Stogumber. Whilst there he had a reckless fling with Mary Gadd, as the result of which she was found to be with child.

At that time children born out of wedlock became the financial responsibility of the local parish, along with the mother. To ensure that such single parent families did not add too great a burden to the ratepayers, parish overseers would

---

8 *The Greenwood Tree* (1984/85), pages 48 & 142, from the researches of Mr L.G. Mead

do all in their powers to ensure such unattached parents became attached in the traditional fashion.

Such was the case with Mary and William. The overseers did everything they could to persuade young William to wed the mother of his unborn child. But William was obdurate. A one night stand was one thing, marriage was another. In no way would he marry this girl.

And so the overseers, after days of unsuccessful coercion, tried a change of tactics. Friendly persuasion over a glass or two of cider became the preferred option. But it didn't stop at a glass or two. The young lad was primed with cider until it was ready to come out of his ears – and then he was carried to the church.

There, ready and waiting, were the vicar and a significant contingent of villagers, there to ensure that their rates remained unaltered. Perhaps someone asked William if he wanted a drop more cider whilst someone else asked if he took this girl to be his lawful wedded bride. Whatever the trigger, he must have said 'I do', and that was it. William Bacon and Mary Gadd were man and wife – and he knew nothing of it!

Imagine his surprise in the morning on waking up next to Mary. Slowly the reality of the situation dawned on him. Initial disbelief turned to panic when the vicar was called in to confirm his actions of the previous day.

William pursued the only option which made sense to him. He ran away and took refuge near Bridgwater where he found himself employment and then kept his head down and commenced an industrious and profitable career, one which brought him thirty years later to operate a grist mill in the village of Spaxton whilst his home was in nearby Durleigh.

Now it so happened that after he deserted Mary Gadd, she moved in with a labourer, Robert Jones, and by the same thirty years on, she had had ten more children by him and (allegedly) someone else. Moreover, one of her daughters was now repeating her mother's history by carrying an illegitimate child of her own. The overseers of Stogumber were once more looking for a solution.

William Bacon had grown in stature and in public recognition as a successful mill operator. His name had reached as far as Stogumber and the next generation of overseers were wondering if this William Bacon could be the one who had deserted their parish thirty years before. They checked the facts – it was the right William Bacon. Problem solved: reunite Bacon with his wife and send all the children with her. Dump them in the parish of Spaxton. But they had to move fast – if the unborn child was delivered in their parish, it would remain their responsibility.

But William Bacon and Robert Jones were also moving with great haste. They met in Stogumber and papers were drawn up confirming the sale by William Bacon of his wife and her four youngest children to Robert Jones for the sum of five shillings. But the authorities were not to be beaten and an order was drawn up by which the family were to be moved to Spaxton, and there the new baby was born. It was Spaxton's turn to pay.

The hoodwinked recruiting sergeant

Yet another story of the deliberate intoxication of an individual, with the sole purpose of hoodwinking him into a course of action he would never otherwise take, comes from Walter Raymond, a great collector of tales of old Somerset.

His account relates to the late 19th century at the time of the revels at Haselbury Pucknett, an event which drew crowds from far and wide. In a festive throng of this kind there were, of course, easy pickings for conmen, pickpockets and recruiting sergeants. It was such a sergeant who arrived in the village dressed in a spanking new red tunic, buttons shining and looking every inch the professional soldier. His dashing figure drew the attention of the ladies – and this was just one of his recruiting techniques. Let the local lads see how attractive the ladies found him in his uniform. They would soon be taking the Queen's shilling, recognition of accepting entry into the service of Her Majesty.

Swaggering down the street, he attracted an entourage of admirers. Seated in the Rose Inn was young George Edwards who, through the open door, could see the procession heading his way. Cursing under his breath, he watched as the sergeant entered the bar and looked straight toward him.

'What a handsome lad!' the sergeant exclaimed and continued the flattery by assuring his target that if he was half as intelligent as the sergeant took him to be, then a young lad like him joining up now could be a corporal in no time and a sergeant like himself before too long. All he needed to do was to take the Queen's shilling.

George, not wishing to be rude, said he'd not object to taking the shilling if he could be convinced that all the sergeant said were true, and not a trick to fool him into enlisting. The sergeant, seizing the opportunity, talked to young George as a son, and called for half a gallon of cider. 'Come on, George. Take the shilling,' he pleaded. 'You'll never regret it.'

George picked up the shilling, considered it for a moment or two, then spat on it for luck and tossed it onto the table to signal a round of drinks at his expense. The sergeant followed with another and the pair drank their fill for an hour until the money had expired. It was now time to reel in the new recruit. The sergeant pinned ribbons of the regimental colours to George's hat and declared it was time for the pair of them to walk out and let the parish see what a splendid recruit he made, prepared as he must be to lay down his life for Queen and country.

George's reluctance to move began to show and the previously most amiable sergeant now developed a sterner, more disciplinarian air. 'Come on, lad. Quick march,' he commanded with the first hint of impatience showing through. By this time quite a crowd had gathered to see if it were true that young George had been recruited into the military. So it was now of face-saving importance for the sergeant that nothing should go wrong. George had to be seen to be going willingly to serve his country.

'OK,' George condescended and looking under the table continued as politely and respectfully as he could, 'but can you just pass up my crutches?' The sergeant bent to look. There beneath the table, tucked out of sight, were George's crutches, just next to George's deformed foot. It was a very red faced sergeant that departed as rapidly and inconspicuously as the gathered throng would allow him.

Man, being reasonable, must get drunk;
The best of life is but intoxication.
George Gordon, Lord Byron, Don Juan II

13

Women Behaving Badly

Walford's Gibbet and Dead Woman's Ditch

The evils of alcohol and its effect on many a marriage have been well understood for countless generations. The basic scenario is much the same in so many cases. The wife stays at home, the husband works and drinks. The family budget is spent on alcohol. The husband, drunk, returns home to a stressed wife and mother unable to make ends meet. An argument ensues. The wife is at the end of her tether. The husband turns to violence and the end of the marriage is nigh. An unusual case is one where it is the wife's drinking that is at the root of the problem. Such an instance was the tragic marriage of John Walford and Jane Shorney who are immortalised on the Quantock Hills at Walford's Gibbet and Dead Woman's Ditch just beyond the village of Nether Stowey.

John Walford followed the calling of a charcoal burner on the Quantock Hills, a solitary existence but suited to this quiet, handsome lad. He was popular in the nearby village of Nether Stowey, especially with Ann Rice, a real local beauty, the miller's daughter to whom he was betrothed. His weeks revolved around a routine of cutting and gathering coppiced timber for burning and then watching over the turf-covered fire whilst the timber slowly smouldered over a period of four to five days. During this time the charcoal burner would tend the fire every hour or two, leaving little time for sleep.

Against the background of this lonely life, Jane Shorney, the daughter of another charcoal burner, turned her attentions to young John. Under cover of darkness, she would visit his secluded hut on the hills, offering him comfort. Inevitably, with John succumbing to the girl's tempting ways, she found herself expecting his child. It was incumbent upon John to forsake his fiancée and marry Jane Shorney. On 18th June 1789 they were wed.

Almost at once, married life became intolerable. Jane taunted John incessantly over the loss of his true love. Her continuous intolerance and vindictiveness reduced him to a shrivelling wreck. Cider was her problem. Drinking as heavily as any man, her behaviour went well beyond that which was reasonable or tolerable. If only John had stayed loyal to Ann.

The situation came to a head on the night of 5th July 1789. By the time John arrived home that evening at the end of his day's work, Jane had already drunk the three quarts of cider that John had been bullied into buying her the previous day. That consumed, she was now looking for more and John offered a shilling which she could take to spend at the Castle of Comfort.

As little as he wanted to go with her, it was late and it was dark. He was concerned for her safety. In addition the Castle of Comfort was frequented by muscular miners from nearby Dodington. Jane's behaviour was already out of control. Further drinking in the presence of such miners was bound to lead to trouble.

The additional drink at the Castle of Comfort added to the ferocity of her attacks on poor John, normally such a tolerant man. She provoked him once too often. On their way home, something snapped inside. He took her by the throat and shook her uncontrollably. Then wrenching a post from the hedge, he beat her unconscious, completing the murderous act by slitting her throat with a knife. Suddenly he realised what he had done. Here was his wife of just seventeen days, limp in his arms. This was no premeditated act. Yes, keep her quiet, remove the source of the torment, but he had no intention of killing her.

Seeing no one was around, and wondering how to dispose of her body, he considered dragging her to a nearby well. The effort was too great, especially disadvantaged as he was with no light to work by. It was all he could do to pull her to an adjacent shallow ditch beneath a small raised bank, the remains of an old Roman settlement. There he placed her in a shallow grave, covered with a few stones, branches and leaves. Inevitably the body would be discovered, buried so inadequately.

Within a few days, it was realised that no one had seen Jane, certainly not since the night of the big argument. Jane's father called for a search party to scour the hills. And there in the remains of that ancient ditch, the body of Jane was later discovered. John admitted his guilt immediately and was taken off to Bridgwater to await his trial. Lord Kenyon presided over the case and, with John Walford's confession, the trial lasted just three hours.

There was no alternative but to declare him guilty and with that came the mandatory death sentence. He was to be hanged by the neck until dead and his body to be given to science. The judge wept as he announced his verdict – a reflection of the compassion he felt for this normally quiet man, driven to the extremes of human tolerance. But the people of Bridgwater had different opinions.

This had been a particularly violent period in Bridgwater's past. Numerous murders had occurred in the preceding years. The public had had enough and required an example to be set. They demanded that John's body should be caged and hung from a gibbet for all to see. That surely would deter any would be villains. The judge acceded to their request.

The following day, John was shackled around the neck, wrists and ankles and placed in a cart for the journey to Nether Stowey and beyond to his place of execution. When he arrived in the village, the preparations at the gibbet were not yet complete and so John's torment was prolonged as the party waited. John was temporarily put into the village lock up and once more cider was to form part of the story. His fellow villagers, feeling much sympathy for the man, provided him with a pint of the local cider, fed by a straw through a small hole in the cell wall.

Local people, as was the custom on such occasions, had turned out in huge numbers in their family groups with their picnics. With the gibbet finally ready for the execution, the horse and cart carrying John arrived.

An excited buzz filled the air as the cart pulled up under the gallows. Then out from the crowd stepped John's first and only true love, Ann Rice. As one, the villagers realised the solemnity of the occasion and turned their backs on the centre stage. Ann walked forward, never taking her eyes off John. The villagers had realised this was Ann's moment to grant John forgiveness. A member of the execution party helped her up onto the cart and for a minute or two they exchanged their final words, no doubt those of regret on the one part and forgiveness on the other.

As Ann leaned forward for a parting kiss, the executioner stepped forward and placed his arm as a barrier between the couple. Ann was quietly and respectfully lifted down from the cart. The horse's rump slapped, the cart pulled forward leaving John's body dancing at the end of the rope.

His remains were put in a cage and left hanging from the 30 foot tall gibbet – that high to ensure its visibility was certain over a wider area – which had been cruelly placed within clear view of the front door of the home of John Walford's mother. The crows, magpies and blowflies having taken what they could from the body, it was eventually buried, still in its cage. The gibbet meanwhile remained in place until the next century when it was taken down and converted into gateposts. Dead Woman's Ditch, a popular meeting place for the Quantock Staghounds, and Walford's Gibbet can still be found on Ordnance Survey maps. And travellers along the A39 between Bridgwater and Minehead will undoubtedly observe a drinking fountain at the roadside near the village of Dodington, erected in memory of Jane Shorney.

> *There are two times when you can never tell what is going to happen. One is when a man takes his first drink; and the other is when a woman takes her latest.*
>
> O. Henry, Octopus Marooned

14

Cider and the Clergy

The relationship between cider and the clergy is almost schizophrenic with the clergy often condemning the consumption of alcohol whilst imbibing large volumes themselves. The essence of that situation is captured nicely in the story of Rogey Nurton who was staggering on his way home from the Acland Hood Arms when he bumped into Vicar Tucker. 'Drunk again!' remarked the vicar as he passed Rogey. 'Yes sir,' replied Rogey, 'and so be I!'

The Diary of a Country Parson

The diaries of James Woodforde do much to illustrate the social character of 18th century rural Somerset. He was a man who enjoyed a drink, had a great interest in food and good company, but frowned on those who took such pleasures in excess, in particular his brother Jack, who seemed destined to be a lifelong alcoholic. However, much of Parson Woodforde's life seemed to revolve around cider and beer.

On 15th January 1764 he had just been appointed as curate at Babcary. Cider was used to bribe the bellringers to welcome his arrival: '*This is the first Sunday I ever officiated at Babcary Church; and I like it very well … I was rung into the parish by Mr. John Bower's order, who gave the Ringers a pail of Cyder on purpose to ring me into the parish.*'

The following week we find that he has '*hired Ned Dyke and his horse to carry some cyder etc. to Babcary for me. I carried three dozen and nine bottles of cyder, and eight bottles of strong beer, with a little jar of pickled oysters, some cheese, and some cold tongue to Babcary, all which were given by my father.*'

In the succeeding year his clerk at Babcary drank so much in an all night session that he failed to make church on Easter Sunday. For this he received a severe lecture from James Woodforde and was then invited to dinner.

By 1767 there are regular accounts of his night-time brewing activities. '*I got up at 3 o'clock this morning to brew a hogshead of strong beer ... I was busy all day at the Lower House, and therefore stayed there the whole day, and did not go to bed this night as we could not tun our liquor till near two in the morning.*'

And his brother seems to benefit greatly from the availability of drink in the house for on 12th February 1770 '*Jack came home a little merry this evening and he laid me a wager of one guinea that he would not from this night get drunk all the year of 1770, that is, as not to be able to tread a Scratch ...*' The following day his brother, unable to walk the scratch, paid up his wager but only to the tune of a sixpenny piece.

His parishioners equally had problems with their drinking habits, for just two weeks later: '*I buried poor Thomas Barnes this afternoon [who had been a long time killing himself by Liquor].*'

Paupers and Pig Killers

William Holland, the vicar of Over Stowey, was another great Somerset diarist and he has given us some wonderful impressions of life in a cider making community in his published diary *Paupers and Pig Killers*. His writings conveniently pick up where Woodforde's leave off, and we are left in no doubt that he had strong views on the quality of Somerset rural folk.

His diary for the final days of October 1799 refers to William Frost and Mr Amen carrying apples to a cart and then to Mr Hewlett's for mashing, pressing and turning into cider. But Mr Hewlett was a user of cheesecloth for the pressing and not straw as was the Somerset tradition. Mr Amen failed to see how anyone could make decent cider using such ideas from outside the county. *'Why Sir, I have made hundreds of hogsheads of cyder in my time,'* declared Mr Amen. *'Silence you Ass,'* responded the vicar. The first pressing complete, the vicar's diary tells how they pressed again to get the water cider. This was clearly a reference to that second pressing from which the weaker cider, or ciderkin, was acquired.

The reverend gentleman also referred to how Mr Amen requested the help of a chap called Robert on the day that William Frost was unable to work. The vicar declined, feeling that the cider makers did little enough as it was. *'Great wages and little work seems to be the general system of this place. The Somersetshire people are of a large size and strong but in my opinion very slow and lazy and discontented and humoursome and very much given to eating and drinking'* ... and later ... *'They were very displeased yesterday when I did not permit my man Robert to idle away his time waiting on them. When I pay people well I expect some work, but the universal system in these parts is a great pay and little work.'* One wonders why he came to Somerset!

After two days at Hewlett's the team had gone to Hurley's to grind another hogshead of cider. *'They will now have their favourite reed instead of the hair bags but things will not be better done.'*

In January 1801 he complains again of the lack of industriousness of his work force and their love of cider when he was having a well excavated. *'Pump business is expensive for they drank gallons beside their pay.'* He was particularly displeased when, after days constructing a ladder inside the well, as the workers brought the very last piece of timber over the well head, the rope broke and the timber dropped, smashing the rungs of the ladder they had just completed as it descended *'so that between eating and drinking they have made a good business of it. These fellows work till late at night and after all their labours left things in a worse state than they found 'em. Men should know what they are about and be prepared with all the instruments proper for the undertaking, but a Somersetshire man is a strange animal, ignorant yet conceited and wonderfully obstinate. He is always wrong in his notions yet thinks no one understands anything but himself.'*

Mishaps in Camerton

The Reverend John Skinner was a diarist who, following in the footsteps of Woodforde and Holland, left us his *Journal of a Somerset Rector 1803–1834.* He served as rector of Camerton in the coal mining area of North Somerset. His was a sad life bestruck with many personal tragedies which no doubt twisted his attitude and left him bitter. Against that background he often begrudged the fun experienced by others, especially when assisted by alcohol.

To hear his criticism of others makes one wonder whether or not a drop ever passed his own lips. But this was a mining and farming community into which he was posted, a community with miners who worked hard and drank hard, and often the two combined in a most tragic mix.

Skinner mentions in his diary for 1804 a miner, Culling Macnab from Ireland, who drowned in the nearby canal after an excess of drink one Saturday night. Aaron Holler's demise was likewise brought on by alcohol. He had spent a night drinking and increasingly became a nuisance by dancing on the tables and being abusive towards his fellow drinkers. It was an evening full of bravado which led to boastful acts of folly. When Aaron left the inn, he went to the Lower Pit and there endeavoured to slide down the rope used to haul coal to the surface. We must assume that in the process of his attempt at breaking the speed record for a rapid descent, his hands would have suffered the severest of rope burns. His momentum would have been such that to slow his descent would necessitate gripping the rope even harder and thus causing even greater burns. In no time at all he was in free fall descent and his body was only discovered when later that evening a mine attendant made the same descent to feed the pit ponies.

The magistrate's blind eye

The son of Robert Paine was once despatched to Camerton's Red Post Inn to fetch a jug of beer for his father. As he left the inn, two locals who had spent four hours drinking there were now on their way home and met the young lad coming out. They drank his father's beer and kicked the jug down the road. So Robert Paine went all the way to Bath to get a summons to have the offenders bound over to keep the peace.

And why should he go to Bath for a summons when there was a local magistrate? Because the local magistrate was the licensee of the inn! Consequently when Isaac Burge, a regular at the inn, was caught robbing a neighbour, he escaped with a fine of £1 7s. For these men were good customers who would drink until four and sometimes six in the morning.

Indeed William Turner drank so much on one such evening that he slept the night on the top of a dung heap adjacent to the inn! All of these misdemeanours were noted in the Revd Skinner's diary, especially that of serving beer on a Sunday when it was officially only permissible to serve travellers.

In 1816, Skinner records how Farmer Sainsbury from Camerton had been into Bath and spent much of the day drinking with a miner by the name of Maine. The two of them made the homeward journey together, both on Sainsbury's overloaded horse. When they arrived at Camerton, Maine's wife was there to greet them. She was fuming, for when Maine left that morning he had sent his horse and cart home in the care of a young lad, far too young in his wife's opinion. And he was clearly now the worse for drink.

Her temper took control and she dragged her errant husband from the horse, causing the saddle to slip down around the horse's girth and tipping Sainsbury out of the saddle. Not satisfied with that, she clearly blamed her husband's condition on Sainsbury and to ensure he was aware of just how angry she was, she took a large stone and smashed out four of his teeth. For this she later appeared before the magistrate who ignored the offence. We can only assume that the magistrate found Sainsbury's behaviour sufficiently intolerable to have justified such an aggressive response from the offended lady, behaviour which provided a salutary warning to other husbands not to overindulge and then look for sympathy from the bench.

Coronation celebration

On the occasion of George IV's coronation, the Camerton bellringers asked the Revd Skinner if he would permit them to ring the church bells in celebration, not least since the neighbouring villages had been ringing all morning. Skinner declared he could see little point in the bells being rung since he was sure the King would not be able to hear them and it only served to keep the villagers away from their work. He was also concerned that the money they would be paid for serving as ringers would be spent on drink. Finally he agreed, but only on condition that the ringers were not to visit the inn but would take their proceeds home immediately to their families.

Such behaviour made him most unpopular with his flock who did much to deride him and it appears that the world and his dog would do their best to deprive him of the money he considered his by right. At tithe collecting time there were always arguments as to whether or not he was charging a fair rate. He would form his own opinion as to what income could be generated from a piece of land and would base the tithe on that no matter how successful or otherwise the farmer had been that particular season.

Even the coal mining company had its problems. The reverend gentleman claimed that when the miners tunnelled beneath land owned by the church, he was entitled to a tithe on the revenue gained therefrom. And so the coal mine owners had to offer their assurances that all of their mine shafts missed the area directly beneath the church land, never actually passing directly beneath it. Believe that if you will!

Problems at the Red Post

But Revd Skinner's real vendetta was against the licensee of the Red Post Inn. Drinking was permitted all hours of the day and night and with no respect shown for the Sabbath. Numerous warnings were issued by Skinner that no good would come from the maintenance of such loose hours. So no doubt he took some satisfaction in attending an inquest which was held at the Red Post into the untimely death of one of its customers.

Farmer Lippeatt had spent several hours drinking at the Red Post on a Saturday evening to the point where he could no longer stand. This also happened to coincide with his money running out. And so when the farmer asked the landlord for a bed for the night, the landlord refused and turfed him out of the front door muttering there was no use asking if he hadn't the means to pay.

And so the poor old farmer, in his drunken haze, made his way along the lane to where he passed through a gap in a hedge which he took to be the road to Dunkerton. Alas it was the road to the quarry and the next twenty feet were spent in free fall descent until he met his end at the bottom of the quarry. A verdict of accidental death was recorded but not without Skinner having his say and perhaps with some justification condemning the landlord for allowing a customer to get to such a state and then to turn him out into the darkness. It was a much closer eye that the local constable kept on the premises for the next few years.

Skinner's diaries provide a remarkable insight into life in the early 19th century with its declining values and poverty, cholera and consumption, pit fatalities and the impoverished meeting a premature end when driven to sheep stealing. It was a period so full of hardships, it was enough to drive anyone to drink.

The wedding at Stanton Drew

The earlier stories give us some idea of how the clergy approached the subject of alcohol. In moderation it was fine and indeed the church had a considerable source of income in brewing church ales as fund raisers. And many a parson brewed both his own beer and cider. But equally they were wise to the controversial aspects of cider when taken in excess. They understood the effect on individuals and families alike and warned against overindulgence. If only the villagers of Stanton Drew had listened to and heeded their wisdom.

Stanton Drew is famous for its three Neolithic stone circles or henges, known as The Wedding. These are found on a prehistoric site and consist of the Great Circle, the Smaller Circle and the Cove. They all resemble lesser versions of Stonehenge. The Great Circle is by the River Chew and was originally some thirty stones.

Legend has it that hundreds of years ago, on a mid-summer's eve, there had been a wedding party in the village church. After the service, the bride, groom and the villagers retired to the barn for the wedding dinner and to make merry. A grand day it was. Enormous volumes of cider were consumed and the musicians played many a jig whilst the villagers danced, laughed and sang.

The bride especially, full of energy, danced like a Dervish as she whirled up and down through the lines of the various sets. More and more cider was 'put away' and the revels grew in reckless abandon. Daylight turned to darkness and the merriment continued well into the night with the party

122

leaving the barn and reconvening in the field alongside the river. Still the bride danced on.

It was a Saturday and midnight approached. These were superstitious and religious people. Under normal circumstances, they knew better than to dance and make merry on the Sabbath. But this was no ordinary night. Spirits were high and the consumption of cider ensured that logic and self respect came well down the list of priorities. As midnight came closer, it was with some reluctance that the majority gathered up their belongings and drifted homeward. But there were many who were willing to stay and continue the joyous celebration. Surely there was no real harm in making merry on a Sunday. The bride in particular begged them all to stay. Have another glass of cider. Dance another reel.

The decision was taken out of their hands when the musicians declared they were not prepared to play and began to leave, being cursed as they did so by the bride. But then, like a knight to the rescue, there arrived a stranger dressed all in black. He offered to play and, after limping slowly to the centre of the circle of dancers, as though with a deformed foot, he began to demonstrate his prowess by taking his fiddle from its case and striking up a jig.

The music was magnificent and soon those who wished to dance were back in action. Some of the villagers began to drift back having heard the enchanting sounds. Others continued their journey home. But each and every enraptured member of the band returned and joined in once more, appreciating the exceptional talents of the unknown stranger.

It wasn't long before one of the party realised the stranger was none other than the devil. As the realisation dawned, they begged in loud cries for the music to stop, but as long as he fiddled they were compelled to dance, increasingly coming under his spell, his for the bidding. It was too late.

In the morning the tragedy of the occasion dawned on those who had made their way home in those safe moments before midnight. They explained how they heard the music begin and how compelling had been the sounds, how it increased in tempo whipping all concerned into a frenzied extravaganza of dance until it faded to be heard no more.

There in the field, where the previous night they had witnessed such gaiety, there now stood the Great Circle of stones, where the dancers had been petrified. The smaller circle showed the spot where the musicians had likewise been entrapped by his spell. And the Cove, a simple group of three stones (actually a chambered long barrow) indicated the parson, the bride and the groom.

For the stranger with the compelling fiddle had been indeed the devil himself who had responded to the appeals of those who wished to ignore the Sabbath and continue their merrymaking. As hangovers go, this has to be the record of all time. Half the village turned to stone.

Should you ever visit the stones at Stanton Drew, just ponder on the lesson to be learned, reflect on this and other stories within these pages. For in each and every case we are justified in saying 'Blame it on the cider!'

Acknowledgements

David Alston, Phil Dolding, Clive Lilley, Mervyn Proctor, Stewart Richards, Duncan Smith, John Sparkes and David Williams for their various stories.

Bibliography

Brown, Donald *Somerset v Hitler* Countryside Books (1999)

Bush, Robin *Somerset Stories* The Dovecote Press (1990)

Evelyn, John *Sylva – Pomona* (1664)

Foot, David *Strange Somerset Stories* Bossiney Books (1984)

Foot, Mark *Cider's Story – Rough and Smooth* Mark Foot (1999)

Holland, William *Paupers and Pig Killers, the diary of William Holland, a Somerset parson, 1799–1818*, Alan Sutton Publishing, edited by Jack Ayres (1984)

Legg, Philippa and Binding, Hilary Somerset *Cider – the complete story* Somerset Books (1986)

Philips, John *Cyder: A poem in two books* (1708)

Raymond, Walter *The Book of Simple Delights* (1906)

Skinner, John *Journal of a Somerset Rector 1803–1834* Oxford University Press (1984)

Sparkes, John *Gi'e I Burtle* Cromwell Press (2001)

Woodforde, James *The Diary of a Country Parson* Oxford University Press (1935)

OTHER TITLES FROM COUNTRYSIDE BOOKS

  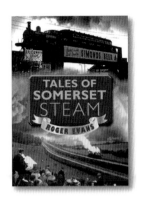

 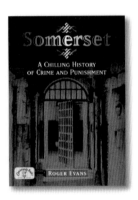 

 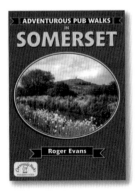 

To see our full range of books please visit
www.countrysidebooks.co.uk

Follow us on @CountrysideBooks